COLLABORATION FOR KIDS

Early-Intervention Tools for Schools and Communities

HEATHERLY WOODS CONWAY, ED.D.

Collaboration For Kids: Early-Intervention Tools For Schools and Communities
© 2006 Heatherly Woods Conway, Ed.D.

    102 pp.

    Bibliography pp. 99–102

    aha! Process, Inc.

    P.O. Box 727

    Highlands, TX 77562-0727

    fax: (281) 421-9852

    www.ahaprocess.com

Copy editing by Mary Conrad Lo and Dan Shenk

Book design by Sara Patton

Printed in the United States of America

ISBN-13: 978-1-929229-71-0

ISBN-10: 1-929229-71-2

U.S. Library of Congress Control Number: 2006933380

10 9 8 7 6 5 4 3 2 1

This book is dedicated to Allyson, Kathryn, Matthew, Erin,
Joshua, and Justin, my wonderful grandchildren.
Every day you inspire my belief in the rights of all children.

Collaboration for Kids

Helping Children Succeed

CONTENTS

Introduction 1

1. Why Bother? 3

2. Collaboration Is a Team Process 11

3. What Is CFK—Collaboration For Kids—Really? 17

4. How Do You Make It Work? 27

5. Setting the Stage for a Pilot Program 33

6. Content and Tips: Getting the Team Ready 43

7. Taking Action: Practical Help for Gathering Resources 51

8. In Conclusion, Let's Begin! 77

Epilogue 83

Using the CD 85

Appendix 87

Bibliography 99

Acknowledgments

As with most projects, this book never would have been written without the important help, inspiration, and encouragement of many people.

To the following scholars, authorities, colleagues, family, and friends, I offer my respect and sincere appreciation:

- Prince William County's Comprehensive Child Study (CCS) specialists Pamela Trapp, Cindy Mandigo, Valerie Sears, Jennifer Dugger, and Kai Munster, for keeping the dream alive

- Judge William Allen Becker, James Rankin, Jane McMorrow, Mary Pitts, Thomas Geib, Paul Borzellino, Keith Sykes, JoAnn Renton, Deborah Carter, and all the participating professionals from their agencies, for recognizing the positive results of true collaboration

- Tom Carter, Jenny Bovard, Pamela Gauch, Lucy Beauchamp, Dr. Edward Kelly, and Dr. Steven Walts, for clearly recognizing the need, as well as the results

- Linda Postelle, for her friendship, caring dedication, hard work, time, and technical assistance

- Michele Conway and Coni Rosati, for their proofreading and insights

- Art Seldney and Michael French, for their friendship and enthusiasm for the project

- My husband, Jack, for his steadfast patience and unconditional encouragement

- My children and grandchildren, who kept me believing in my work

In addition, I offer special thanks to Dr. Ruby Payne, for encouraging me to pursue this project.

INTRODUCTION

If we are to reach real peace in the world,
we shall have to begin with the children.

–Mohandas K. Gandhi
Indian philosopher and social activist

Much has been written about children with special needs and challenges. Recently, the "No Child Left Behind" legislation has stimulated a lively national debate on education and standardized testing. Of utmost urgency however, is that we look carefully at the increasing number of children who are "unavailable to learn"—unavailable because of adverse societal and family influences that can sometimes bring the learning process to a halt.

This book describes a simple, straightforward initiative—Collaboration For Kids (CFK)—that can be put into place in any community by a single school, school division, human service agency, or any caring and interested individual. It outlines an interactive process for addressing, early in a child's life, problems that negatively impact education—a process that utilizes the inner strengths of the child and family members. Guidelines for training in the not-so-natural art of collaboration are given, and the CFK training program is clearly portrayed.

Some truly serious children's issues are, unfortunately, unattractive political fodder in the U.S. Therefore, these very critical problems rarely receive adequate, realistic levels of funding or attention. Current legislative initiatives in education are really not new educational concepts. In general, the *integrated* needs of the *whole* child, particularly those of the "unavailable child"—a rapidly expanding population, are not adequately addressed. By ignoring this omission, we as a society may be positioning ourselves to deal with increasingly troubled communities and an undereducated populace in the future. If agencies and schools continue to work in isolation, progress made toward the goal of developing healthier, more educated children and families will remain at current levels.

What can be done? The need is not for more research! The need is for true collaborative community interaction among schools and human service agencies to help stabilize families and place children back on the path to successful learning.

This book is written as it was lived in order to bring a real message and real solutions to readers. As I travel and tell others about CFK, I am frequently asked if I have written about the program so it could be started in other jurisdictions. I am doing this now because of these requests, and because I believe passionately in the right of every child to be safe, nurtured, and educated.

–Heatherly Woods Conway, Ed.D.

WHY BOTHER?

Few will have the greatness to bend history itself;
but each of us can work to change a small portion
of events, and in the total of all those acts
will be written the history of this generation.

–Robert F. Kennedy
U.S. attorney general

Throughout the United States, demands placed on schools and community systems are rising rapidly because of increasingly adverse social conditions. More and more children come to school *unavailable to learn*, with their "emotional quotients" (Goleman, 1995) and intellectual quotients (Cryan, 1985) depressed because of problems experienced in their lives outside the classroom.

Figures for 2003 from the Children's Defense Fund (*National Kids Count: A Data Book*) give us chilling information.

Each day in America …

- 2,385 babies are born into poverty.

- 13,245,000 children live in poverty.

- 77 children die before their first birthday.

- 2,482 children are found to be abused or neglected.

- 4 children are killed by firearms.

- 4,262 children are arrested.

- 177 children are arrested for violent crimes.

- 1,186 babies are born to teen mothers.

- 2,756 high school students drop out of school.

- 16,964 public school students are suspended.

- 9,977,000 school children speak languages other than English as their first language.

- 8,391,000 children do not have health insurance.

- 5 children or teens commit suicide.

- 50–75% of incarcerated juveniles have diagnosable mental health disorders.

In *A Framework for Understanding Poverty,* Ruby Payne quotes these statistics:

- In 2003 the poverty rate for individuals under age 18 in the United States was 17.6% (U.S. Bureau of the Census, 2004).

- Regardless of race or ethnicity, poor children are much more likely than non-poor children to suffer developmental delay and damage, to drop out of high school, and to give birth during the teen years (Miranda, 1991).

- The United States' child poverty rate is substantially higher—often two to three times higher—than that of most other major Western industrialized nations.

The National Incidence Study on Child Abuse and Neglect (Sedlak and Broadhurst, 1996) documents an enormous increase nationally in these tragedies, noting as prime causal factors the use of illicit drugs and economic stressors. Also reported is the fact that investigations into maltreatment of children have fallen dramatically as child protective agencies across the country have reached operational capacity. Sedlak and Broadhurst find further that, as a result, children in the United States are not receiving adequate protection. The study suggests that neglect warrants more concentrated attention overall, as it often leads to abuse. The authors conclude that greater collaborative efforts are needed on behalf of these children.

The child experiencing trauma has been described in the literature as "vigilant yet anesthetized." Garbarino and his associates describe children who, after exposure to various types of violence, exhibit passive reactions and regressive symptoms, such as enuresis, delayed adaptive behaviors, aggression, increased inhibition, somatic complaints, cognitive distortions, and learning difficulties. The impact of family and community dysfunction on appropriate development is well-documented by these researchers: Truancy, lowered cognitive ability, interruptions in social/emotional development, delayed physical development, delays in emergence of speech and language, inappropriate behavioral manifestations, and other developmental anomalies are cited as consequences for children (Garbarino, et al., *Children in Danger,* 1992).

"America's fight against violence must begin in the high chair, not the electric chair," states George Sweat, former police chief and now Secretary of the Department of Juvenile Justice and Delinquency Prevention for the state of North Carolina. Edward Flynn, former Arlington County police chief and current Police Commissioner for Springfield MA has indicated that domestic violence involving children will not be reduced until the government's investments in prisons and police are matched by front-end investments for programs specific to children's well-being. Another group of investigators concludes that unavailable, neglectful, and/or abusive parents often present a direct threat to a child's physical, emotional, and intellectual development (Kurtz, et al., 1993).

The 1995 Gallup Poll reported that 49 out of every 1,000 children are physically abused and that 19 out of every 1,000 are sexually abused. In 2005 the U.S. Department of Health & Human Services (DHHS) released statistics revealing that of the 2.9 million cases of child abuse reported in 2003 (three-quarters of whom were under the age of 4), 906,000 were investigated to the point of substantiating abuse or neglect: 1,500 of these children died. Tragically, other DHHS statistics indicate that the majority of children who died due to abuse or neglect were never brought to the attention of a child protection agency.

If we are to embrace early collaborative intervention for children in our communities, we must actively address such issues as significant increases in:

- The number of "working poor"
- Cases of domestic violence and child abuse
- The number of homeless individuals
- Gang violence
- Parent and student substance abuse and trafficking
- Mental health disorders that impact children and families

The tremendous problems faced by those not proficient in the English language must not be overlooked. These factors are real deterrents to learning that must be recognized and dealt with by all communities. Schools everywhere can be leaders in this effort, since children usually spend more hours per day being seen and attended to by school personnel than they spend at home in the care of their parents. Schools, however, must have on their side the collaborative power of community human service agencies and/or religious organizations if real solutions are to be found for children.

After examining these powerful statistics, and with the knowledge that we *can* make a difference in the lives of children and their families, the *why* in "why bother" becomes clear. We must move forward toward empowering parents to be leaders and problem solvers—agents of change in their own lives, the lives of their children, and their communities. Collaboration For Kids provides an opportunity for parents to become those leaders in planning for the education of their children and the future stability of their families and communities.

THE CFK STORY

This is the story of a large school system in one of the fastest-growing counties in the nation—and how it is successfully meeting the needs of children who are *unavailable to learn* due to problems experienced outside of school. Prince William County, Virginia, has a school system that is opening new schools every year. It has evolved from a quiet rural system into an enormous urban school division serving more than 66,000 children in 80-plus schools. It's a county filled with the questions, concerns, and challenges that so many urban areas have today. The school division is constantly wrestling with the best ways to meet the educational needs of its large and diverse population. As with most areas of the United States, Prince William County has experienced the rise in social dysfunction that goes hand in hand with rapid growth and other trends of the times. With escalating levels of family, community, and educational problems, the school division and the community's poorly funded social agencies are constantly searching for ways to stabilize families and educate the population.

In 1998, I—acting as a single individual within the school division—started Comprehensive Child Study (CCS), the first CFK initiative, in Prince William County. (The name CCS was chosen to support Virginia's 1993 legislative action on behalf of children titled the "Comprehensive Services Act.") CCS proved to be a highly successful way of addressing the community's challenges while simultaneously ensuring that children were educated and families stabilized. An initial pilot program was put into place in three elementary schools. Within six years, and with remarkable success, it had spread to 39 elementary schools. During the 2004–05 school year, more than 1,550 children in 44 elementary schools made outstanding progress as participants in CCS Team Action Plans. This award-winning* program—a simple, effective process having an 89% success rate—has had a dynamic impact on the children and families in this district.

A Juvenile Court judge in Prince William County wrote a letter on behalf of all the district judges stating that it was their belief that the effectiveness and success of the CCS (CFK) program had led to a significant reduction in the number of middle and high school students coming through the court system (see letter in Appendix).

COLLABORATION FOR KIDS: OUTCOMES/RESULTS

- Reduced truancy and tardiness

- Increased parental empowerment, participation, responsibility, and guided follow-through

- Improved academic progress

- Fewer classroom disruptions

- Improved behavior

- Reduced referral to special education

- More appropriate use of community services facilitated

- Reduced recidivism rate

- Possibly reduced number of middle and high school students in the court system.

- Stabilized children and families

- Successful, ongoing collaboration and communication between schools and agencies

- And more

* 1. Prince William County Award for Outstanding Team Performance
2. Prince William County United Way Special Recognition Award
3. Virginia Governor's Conference on Education Recognition

CCS was designed to be an "early" intervention program for children of preschool age through Grade 5, the definition of "early" being early in life, not necessarily in the early stages of existing problems. One of the assumptions made initially was that this program would make big differences in truancy and tardiness. With minimal research, it was determined that preschool and elementary-grade patterns of truancy and tardiness are symptoms indicating the presence of underlying family dysfunction. An informal study in the first three CCS (CFK) schools indicated that, in all but two cases (where illness was a key), underlying family dysfunction was at the core of truancy. Children in this age range usually love attending school.

NOTE: *Good results are based on interventions that take place early in the lives of children.*

SAM

Sam (not his real name) was a 9-year-old fourth-grader who had two very young male siblings. He was frequently late for school and often came without his homework, appearing tired and inappropriately dressed for the weather. His mother came to school periodically to complain loudly about things that did not make sense to school officials, but she never appeared for scheduled parent conferences. The teacher expressed concerns about the mother's mental health status, as she always seemed to be too hostile to be able to engage in discussions. When the mother did arrive at school in anger, she often had bruises and scratches on her arms, face, and neck.

One day I entered the school building only to be greeted by a flurry of confused words from Sam's teacher, the principal, and others. Once calmed, the teacher explained that I must speak to Sam immediately; he had arrived at school very early that morning, before the building was open, having walked the two miles from home in his bare feet. He had two black eyes and was limping. Everyone had tried to provide comfort and find out what had happened, but Sam said he had to talk to me. Someone had found spare shoes and socks, and he was waiting for me in my office. I was concerned, as I had met with Sam many times and knew him well. As I entered, he looked at me with stern eyes and said with some assurance, "All right, do you want me to tell you what my mom said to tell you, or do you want to know what happened?" Suddenly he burst into tears, and that stern gaze faded into hopelessness. He kept repeating, "I really tried, and I didn't do anything bad. Do you believe me?" Once consoled, he described, step by step, what had happened. To make a long story short: His mother had made him responsible for feeding both his siblings—an infant and a 2-year-old brother—before he could go to school, while she sat on the couch drinking. The 3-month-old was on the floor crying and Sam was trying to get the 2-year-old to eat some cereal. Mom didn't like the crying and said Sam wasn't working fast enough. As Sam went over to pick up the baby, his mother grabbed him and punched him in both eyes. Sam said he almost dropped the baby, and then tripped trying to get away from his mother, hurting his leg. He put the baby back on the floor and started to go to heat up a bottle when his mother grabbed him again. He escaped, running out the door with his mother shouting after him, then ran to school, where he knew he would be safe.

Of course, this became a child protection case. During the first social services visit, both younger siblings were taken to the hospital for complete examinations. The infant was suffering from "failure to thrive" syndrome and the 2-year-old had pneumonia. After two weeks in the hospital, both were placed back with the mother. Sam was temporarily removed from the home twice; following additional abusive incidents, he was permanently removed. The baby and 2-year-old remained with the mother.

Some of the questions raised by Sam's case are:

- Could this have been averted with an early-intervention protocol in place?

- How could Sam, already behind in school, concentrate on his work that day?

- How many of Sam's classmates were negatively impacted by his patterns of tardiness, ongoing stress behaviors, and incomplete work?

- How much time was taken from Sam's classmates as the teacher tried to help him catch up academically and worked individually with his behaviors?

- Without regular, steady intervention, what will likely happen to his two younger siblings?

- Should a collaborative system designed to help the parent realize and express problems—and to plan for family success—have been in place?

It's quite obvious that Sam's story is only one of a multitude, illustrating just a few of the many serious issues confronting young children. Sam's predicament went unresolved for quite some time, having many twists and turns that greatly affected all three children in the home. Stories like Sam's are all too common.

Looking beyond the tragedies of abuse and domestic violence, we find many other factors in children's lives that become deterrents to learning. There are adults who, depressed due to external circumstances, become inert and unable to parent; families who are living in substandard environments without water or food; families who experience chronic illnesses that impact the children; families experiencing unemployment and language barriers; and families having low tolerances for stress who find themselves in highly stressful work positions that leave little time or emotional capacity to cope with problems that arise in the children's educational settings.

My point here is that we know these stressors are occurring in children's lives on a daily basis. One child in a devastating situation is one child too many, but the fact is that the United States has many Sams for whom the safest, most secure time of each day will be spent in school. Individuals not involved in education or human services work often find it easy to put an unpleasant subject of this nature out of mind. This is done far too often by far too many who could, if they so desired, make a difference. If statistics are needed, they certainly can be provided: The research has been done over and over again through the years. Even so, the number of families lacking stability and appropriate parenting skills —families who are no longer able to recognize their own amazing strengths and resources—is now rapidly rising. Without having a plan in place to address this dismal situation, the wealthiest, most productive nation in the world simply perpetuates a cycle of dysfunction and underachievement, a cycle that compromises children, the workforce, and society itself. This isn't a prediction, it's reality. And it's now time to move forward.

COLLABORATION IS A TEAM PROCESS

It takes a village to raise a child.

–Nigerian proverb

The CCS/CFK program involves a collaborative "Team" approach. This means that the agency and school representatives concerned must first learn the *process* of collaborating in order to participate as Team players. The role of each Team player is crucial to the ultimate success of the child and family, and *communication is the key element.*

Historically, agencies and school divisions have worked together, but not as a collaborative team with shared goals. The school division has its own individual mandate (educating children), as has each separate agency involved. This can often work well for some children. In today's complex world, however, truly collaborative efforts will be much more likely to reap the kinds of benefits needed. We quickly discovered that collaboration is not necessarily a natural process. It is a taught skill. If we are to work together optimally, certain criteria must be in place, and we must be trained based on these criteria.

In our initial training together we first needed to define "collaboration." For the purposes of CFK, we did so in this way:

> *Collaboration is a process to achieve goals that cannot be reached acting alone (or at least cannot be reached as well). Collaboration is a means to an end and not an end in itself. The desired goal is improved outcomes for children and families.*

It's important here to note that the *parent* is the primary stakeholder—Team member—in the collaboration. Trusting that help is on the way, parents often come into this collaborative process feeling depressed, inert, over-emotional, and anxious. With this in mind, all other Team members are trained in the art of, and take responsibility for, being productive listeners rather than lecturers. Stories are told and there is lots of conversation, but lecturing and judgmental declarations have no place here. Team members become "co-investigators" with the parent(s);

> In 1992 Charles Brener said, "If collaboration is to result in more responsive services to children and families, it must do more than redesign organizational flow charts. Collaboration is too important a concept to trivialize in this fashion. Its goal is the alleviation of children's very real needs."

that is, everyone becomes a problem solver and everyone, then, has something to offer (DeVol, 2004). One major goal of this collaborative process is helping the parent emerge as a goal setter and leader, first on the Team, then in the family, and finally in the community. With this emergence, of course, comes progress for the child.

Because this isn't a "quick fix" program, and because the *parent* guides the Team to the point of change, each family remains an active part of the Team for as long as necessary to complete the plan and move ahead. Therefore, as *parent-guided* Teams, we become active in reducing the recidivism rate in communities we serve. In some states a variation of this approach is called "Wraparound."

Agency and school participants in a CFK program will vary from jurisdiction to jurisdiction. The wonderful advantage of this program is that it's flexible enough to accommodate a wide range of needs—from the largest school district to the very smallest. To establish collaborative partners for the first CCS Team in Prince William County, I (a school social worker at the time) started with a friend and enthusiastic colleague at the Community Services Board; this agency was home to the appropriate mental health services. Then I added the Department of Social Services, the Juvenile Court Services Unit, and our Virginia Cooperative Extension Office to my list.

NOTE: When getting started, it's worth exploring land grant colleges or universities to see if a Cooperative Extension Office already exists, because such offices offer a wealth of services, including parenting classes, financial planning assistance, and home-buying assistance, among others.

Following a meeting with an interested staff member, and then the director, each of these agencies agreed to participate in our new collaborative venture. Because this was a pilot program involving only three schools, no agency was overburdened, nor did anyone involved have any idea of its eventual growth and ultimate success. It seemed a relatively simple thing.

After proving its worth, the program grew each year. By the second year it was apparent that we needed to implement formal training of community stakeholders, establish firm protocols, and develop some forms and organizational structure. Although the actual training process will be discussed later, it's worth noting that we trained more than 175 participants from many professions in the second year.

Among our trainees were the following:

- School personnel, including elementary guidance counselors, principals, assistant principals, central office administrators, school social workers, school psychologists, school nurses, safety and security officers, and truancy officers

- Mental health workers from the Community Services Board

- Court services personnel and judges

- Social workers from Social Services

- Virginia Cooperative Extension personnel

- Police Department personnel

- Public Health personnel

- Domestic Violence Coalition workers

- Pediatric Primary Care Project personnel (children's health insurance project)

- Volunteer Emergency Families for Children personnel (volunteer respite care providers)

- CASA volunteers (court-appointed special advocates for children)

As we realized that the program itself will always be a work-in-progress, due to turnover in agencies and schools and the changing nature of social structures, it became clear that training needed to become an ongoing part of our responsibility. Each year, as we have added schools to the program, training sessions have been implemented in those schools.

Twice-yearly meetings are conducted with agency directors and area judges to keep them informed of the program's parameters and progress. At this writing (late 2005) we have trained more than 500 individuals; they are now helping children in 44 elementary schools. CFK continues to grow.

What Are the Elements of Collaboration?

Prior to reviewing the mandated purpose of a CFK program, such as CCS, we need to establish the tenets of, and barriers to, any discussion or teaching of collaboration.

Collaborators must first agree on the fact that there is a *need* for the collaboration—and, certainly, prior research and firsthand experience will inform this discussion. Once in agreement about the need, a *common goal* must be established. *Shared professional knowledge* of the other agencies and participants is necessary in order for a *common professional language* to be created. *Shared responsibility and accountability,* as well as *shared resources and rewards,* must be agreed upon from the outset; and *open, positive communication, to include trained productive listening,* becomes foundational to the collaborative effort.

ELEMENTS

Recognized need

Shared goal

Shared professional knowledge

Common professional language

Shared responsibility and accountability

Shared resources

Shared reward

Open, positive communication/productive listening

For these elements to become real and a part of the forward action, stakeholders need to discuss and commit to:

- A professional and emotional shift of consciousness

- A release of territorial ideas

- A release of personal barriers

- A commitment to make a difference

Possible barriers to collaboration that must be carefully considered include:

- Negative past experiences with collaboration efforts in the community

- Difficult past or present relationships among potential member organizations

- Competition, or turf issues, between/among potential Team members

- Personality conflicts between representatives of member organizations

- Racial or cultural polarization in a community or organization

- Differing community or organizational norms and values about cooperation

As individuals sharing a goal, we must grasp the concept that community collaboration works best when it's open to the richness brought by individual members of the community's different cultural, racial, ethnic, and income groups. By recognizing the commonality of all human beings and treasuring the uniqueness of various cultures, not only do we affirm our own internal wealth, we also ensure both our own growth and the success of the collaboration. Sometimes the scope of diversity existing in an entire school presents seemingly insurmountable challenges, but after examining each child on a case-by-case basis, collaborative Team Action Plans can be individualized to meet the unique needs of each child and family. This freedom to supply individual solutions within a diverse group grants us the gifts of new perspective and creative thinking as we address our communities' needs.

> **During training, or as a precursor to training, have stakeholders write about those things that make them skeptical or give them negative feelings regarding the collaborative effort. Often this feedback makes planning and communication easier as the process is explored. Another effective question at the outset might be: "Where would you rather be than at this meeting?!"**

To avoid pitfalls, it's important to:

1. Keep the commitment focused by defining a simple goal

2. Really get to know other members

3. Encourage clear communication and negotiation

4. Be transparent and straightforward about your needs and the needs of others in the collaboration

5. Clearly define roles

Earlier, we spoke of moving forward. That takes action! From this point on, I will provide some *forward actions* at the end of each chapter.

Forward Actions

- Assess the personal enthusiasm and resources you bring to this vital endeavor.

- Examine those resources, listing them in the following categories: mental, emotional, physical, support systems, compensatory skills, and relationships.

- List supportive personal relationships that you know you can count on as you approach this work.

- List reliable professional acquaintances who might be interested in exploring this program with you.

- Study the primary tenets of collaboration to strengthen your knowledge of this process.

- *Act* by making a written list of your first agency contacts.

What Is CFK—
Collaboration For Kids—Really?

Education must not simply teach work—
it must teach life.

–W.E.B. DuBois
Author and civil rights leader

A CFK program is an intervention by a collaborative, trained, multi-agency Team occurring early in the life of the child who is "unavailable to learn" due to non-academic environmental factors, such as physical abuse, substance abuse, and deterioration of mental health, among many others. The program formalizes an effort to help these children and their families navigate existing difficulties by facilitating access to services, support systems, and relationships, thereby preventing in large measure the need for future protective, punitive, or treatment interventions. CFK represents an effort to ensure that the child is safe, nurtured, and educated. Key to this collaboration is empowerment of the parent to emerge as a leader in the process and, therefore, in the life of the child, as family functioning is strengthened.

When parents choose not to participate in this growth and leadership opportunity to help their child, CFK nonetheless functions as a proactive, effective process ensuring that definitive action still is taken to promote the safety and well-being of the child.

CFK Team meetings take place in the school after all standard school accommodations and interventions have been tried without success. The meetings proceed according to a planned, coordinated protocol, with all stakeholders— ideally including the parent(s)—present.

The purpose of CFK is to prevent the need for future social services, court, police, and mental health interventions because of gross errors in judgment, truancy, criminal acts, or other maladaptive behaviors due to serious disturbance on the part of a child or family members.

A key premise of CFK is that a child who is currently "unavailable to learn" can be helped to acquire appropriate learning skills and life skills through the collaborative efforts of school, parent(s), and community service agencies. It is our belief that the "unavailable" state frequently has its origin in problems occurring outside of the school environment, in the home, or elsewhere.

One mandate for CFK is to facilitate development of parental strengths in directions that will benefit child, family, and community. By acting on this mandate, we help children become successful learners and, ultimately, productive citizens in the community.

"Who Is This Child?"

The child who is "unavailable to learn" does not respond to standard school interventions and has "red flag" behavioral problems, some of which are noted on the next page.

Abby

Abby (not her real name) was a shy and quiet fifth-grade girl. Her delicate, very slight features and blond hair made her look somewhat angelic; however, her eyes appeared sad and she seldom smiled. She was a hard worker in school, but it was apparent that her mind often wandered. She tended to flinch when children or adults spoke loudly, and hardly ate a thing during the school day, though she always bought her lunch. Abby's grades were sliding downward. She was without friends in the classroom, mostly because she kept very much to herself.

Abby's parents were contacted on several occasions and finally made themselves available for a conference by telephone. They understood that Abby's grades were slipping and agreed to put measures in place at home to address this problem. Her parents both worked for the same high-tech corporation and had very "important" jobs. It was clear that their time was very valuable; it also seemed evident that Abby's school situation wasn't their first priority.

Abby's brother, a junior in high school, often picked her up at the end of the school day. Abby's teachers got to know him somewhat; though he was caring toward his sister, they were concerned about putting Abby in the car with him because there was some visual evidence that he might be involved with alcohol

'RED FLAG' BEHAVIORS

- Truancy

- Patterns of tardiness

- "Acting out" or withdrawn behaviors

- Knowledge of, or conversation about, sex and drugs inappropriate for the child's age or stage of development

- Delays in common adaptive-behavior skills

- Lower-than-expected academic performance

- Inability to build or maintain appropriate peer and/or adult relationships

- Anxiety, fearfulness, flinching

- Inability to cope with transitions during the school day

- Lethargy, sleeping at school

- Hunger

- Poor hygiene

- Encopresis, enuresis, or unusual toileting habits

- Unusual eating habits or patterns

- Somatic complaints

- Lack of parental interest in child's basic health or school performance

- And many others

and, possibly, drugs. This was discussed with the parents, who professed no knowledge of any such involvement.

As Abby's parents began applying pressure at home, she began to unravel. In the classroom she appeared to be tired. Abby complained of stomach aches and headaches. She didn't want to go home at the end of the day. She stated that home was just too hard; her brother had been instructed by their parents to see to it that Abby stayed in her room each day after school until they got home at 7 o'clock. Abby grew increasingly anxious, and the parents became increasingly unavailable. At the school's Child Study meeting the teacher asked that the case be referred to CFK.

RONNIE

Ronnie (not his real name) was a 200-pound third-grade boy with a heart as big as he was. Having missed 51 days of school the previous year, he was on his way to doing the same thing again. Sweet-natured most of the time, he was teased and subtly tormented by other students, most of whom were older. His mother, a single parent with a live-in boyfriend, wasn't very tolerant of Ronnie's problems: When school officials asked for the fourth time that Ronnie be checked medically, she finally took him to the doctor. A cursory physical exam was completed with no remarkable results; the mother was given a diet for Ronnie to follow.

The mother tried to comply with the diet, but Ronnie resisted. He began to hoard candy, cookies, and other sweets under his bed, then ate to his heart's content when alone. Within two weeks of the doctor's visit, Ronnie was found unconscious and in a coma. The diagnosis of diabetes was made for the first time. He was in the hospital for three months. When he came home the mother tried to restrict his diet appropriately and give him his various medications. Ronnie fought the regimen and found himself back in the hospital. After Ronnie came home the second time, his mother announced she couldn't manage her son's illness or get him to come back to school. The case was referred to CFK.

RESULTS

These referrals to the CFK program turned into great success stories for both children. With Ronnie's mother as a capable assessor and planner, the CFK Team was able to draw up an Action Plan with the adults in the household—and to get home-based services in place to help restructure the home to meet Ronnie's new needs. Home-based counseling was provided. With this support, along with renewed healthy relationships, the family became able to recognize its own built-in strengths and resources. A visiting nurse provided in-home diabetes education and helped Ronnie recognize his own role in feeling better about himself.

During the first year the Team's Action Plan found a healthier Ronnie attending school regularly *and* making good academic progress. Ronnie's mother—with the encouragement of those around her, including Ronnie's doctor, coupled with her newly found leadership skills—started a support group for parents of chronically ill children. Twenty moms now meet together every week.

Through the work of a CFK Team Action Plan, Abby's parents were able to recognize their need for family counseling. Some of the outcomes of this were: alcohol abuse treatment for the brother; a new job, with a less stressful timetable, for the mother; a mellowed attitude regarding family time for the father; and a new emphasis on participation in Abby's school challenges. In addition to family counseling, Abby received individual therapy, some of which included play and art. Abby was able to express fear of her brother's behaviors and her need for more nurturance and time from her parents.

These positive results can be attributed to the fact that all Team members understood the need for listening, co-investigation (DeVol, 2004), modeling, and support. Each Team member, including the parent, followed through with responsibilities delineated in the Plan, such as referral, assessment, telephone support, and medical contact. The school Team member kept things moving by doing the case tracking and record keeping. The parents and children were never left hanging, as there was always someone to contact. Parents were given models and encouragement, eventually becoming good evaluators of their own situations and, therefore, Team leaders.

THE DESIGN

If we were to picture CFK, it might look like the diagram on the next page. The parent is an integral part of the Team, and the child and family are the focus. We see the child and family encircled with helpers from agencies who are all there for the sole purpose of listening and co-investigation with the parent—in order to define the issues that are preventing the child from learning. With the parent's input primary, a workable Team Action Plan is put together. Any already existing support systems the family may have are utilized, and others are added if appropriate. The same Team members stick with the parent throughout the Plan's implementation, providing stable relationships and encouraging forward

SCHOOLS

1. Team

Schools
Social services
Court services
Mental health
Child Parents Family
Parents
Cooperative extension
Others as needed

2. Team Action Plan

Goal setting
Structure
Referrals & services
Voice
Child Parents Family
Support
Modeling
Relation-ships
Monitoring

3. Established Outcomes

Reduced truancy
Safer com-munity
Improved behaviors
Family stabilization
Child Parents Family
Efficient use of services
Reduced juvenile crime
Increased classroom teaching time
Academic progress

action. This can mean anywhere from eight weeks to two or three years. Each participating agency has several trained specialists dedicated to being part of CFK Teams in the schools every week.

As shown in Circle 1, it's important to note that a specific array of trained personnel will be needed, depending on the situation. In cases of domestic violence, a domestic violence counselor who has been trained in the CFK process may need to be called in. There will be times when a person from the health department or the police department is needed—or someone from CASA (court-appointed special advocates), the local shelter program, or even the family's private therapist or doctor.

Circle 2 describes the individual Team Action Plan formulated for each case under parent leadership, with support and resource information from the other Team members. This Plan provides referrals and contact assistance for services such as:

- Home-based counseling
- Coordination of, and referral to, medical services
- Respite services
- Therapeutic respite

- Daycare
- Parenting classes
- Legal assistance
- Financial resources
- Others as needed

Support systems and relationships are formed as the applicable services are monitored by Team members. In effect, a "voice" is provided for the issues, the actions, and the family's strengths and weaknesses. Support and structure are continually available. Appropriate visual and behavioral models are utilized, and appropriate language and life skills are demonstrated, helping the family move forward to a better place. Shared responsibility on the part of Team members is key to a family's success. *NOTE: It's important to keep in mind that the term "Team members" includes the parent(s).*

Circle 3 illustrates some successful outcomes of a functioning Team Action Plan. As family members work together with the help of Team members, they begin to realize that support for inner (and access to outer) resources is available. Delicately balanced family stabilization takes place as a new sense of safety and security emerges for each family member. Parents, feeling new leadership capabilities, strength, and courage, begin to plan and set goals, putting new family structures and systems into place. The concepts of nurturance of child *and* self grow and stabilize. A realization of the importance of the child's education emerges.

Of interest is the broader impact of such collaboration. As you can see in the diagram below, there's a communitywide payoff for this kind of intervention. At school there are fewer classroom disruptions, increasing teaching time for the rest of the children, thereby increasing overall access to education. There are improvements in school attendance: less truancy and tardiness. Positive communication enhances parental investment in the child's education. Parents become constructive leaders in the school and community. Prince William County's Juvenile Court judges believe that the reduction in their workload may well have been due to the introduction of CFK (see judge's letter, Appendix). The end result is a healthier, safer community with better educated citizens who are more adequately prepared for the workplace.

ESTABLISHED OUTCOMES

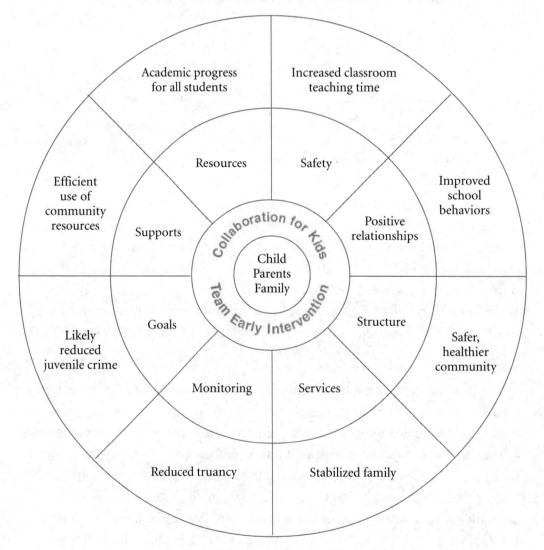

Collaboration For Kids differs from programs that have historically placed community agencies and services physically into the schools to take referrals and work cases. CFK *joins all relevant agencies together with the parents* to listen, facilitate, and plan—to support family members over the long term as they make lifelong changes that ultimately will benefit the larger community. Each Team Plan can be collaboratively supported for as long as necessary to ensure that the focus remains clear, that parents have utilized strengths for leadership toward change, and that stabilization has occurred for child and family. Both short-term and long-term planning and implementation *really happen*.

FORWARD ACTIONS

- Build your knowledge of community resources (make a notebook or file).

- Using your resource file and your personal and professional relationships, decide who you would place in Circle 1 of the design diagram.

- Most agencies have a number of active programs. Explore program options available from your primary agencies, keeping a record of them in your resource file.

- Explore programs outside of the primary agencies. Does the closest land grant college or university offer a Cooperative Extension Program that would benefit families?

- Contact volunteer and 501(c)3 non-profit programs and organizations in your community to determine what services or benefits they offer.

How Do You Make It Work?

*We must always go the second mile. When we go
the first mile, we simply do what is required of us.
It is when we go the second mile that excellence
is achieved and minor miracles happen.*

–Deborah McGriff
U.S. superintendent of schools

Years of Promise: A Comprehensive Learning Strategy for America's Children, a report funded by the Carnegie Task Force on Learning in the Primary Grades (1994), states that schools alone cannot meet the goals for learning and achievement that children must accomplish to succeed. It states that all community institutions must contribute positively to children's learning and development in order to help reverse patterns of underachievement. Historically, individual community agencies have worked in isolation. Here we describe another paradigm: *collaboration*.

The CFK process begins after the teacher and administrator have had discussions with the parent and the school-based Child Specific Team (or Child Study Committee), and a child is referred. The referral takes place after standard accommodations and assistance available in the school have been tried without success. The school committee has kept a record of the child's strengths, the committee's concerns, and any recommendations. Committee members have documented what accommodations have worked, as well as which have not worked. If the regular Child Study Committee or the parent feels that further action is needed—and also feels that external issues (at home) are having a negative impact on the child's learning—the case is referred to CFK.

If a parent chooses not to participate in the CFK process, several options are offered, depending on the nature of the case. These might include a one-on-one meeting with the CFK specialist in order to clarify the process and encourage the parent. Often a home visit involving careful listening will build the bridge into the CFK process, which is always the goal. If a parent, over time, continues to choose not to cooperate, and any danger to the child is suspected, appropriate steps are taken immediately.

However, when a cooperative family is referred to the CFK specialist, an intake form is completed and a permission form is signed by the parent. [See Chapter 7: In Prince William County we use a "universal" permission (Consent to Release and Exchange Information) form, one that has been approved by legal counsel for all relevant county agencies. This makes possible an open exchange of information among Team members.] At this point the CFK specialist schedules a Team meeting in the school. This will include school professionals who know the child best, the appropriate agency representatives, and the parent as primary Team member. Minutes of the meeting are kept, and after discussion, a Team Action Plan is put into writing. As an integral part of the Plan, each Team member, including the parent, agrees to the role he or she will play. The next meeting date is scheduled, and a monitoring process begins. The parent, with the guidance and support of Team members, can now assume leadership in implementing the Plan.

In her book *A Framework for Understanding Poverty,* Dr. Ruby Payne speaks about the many resources a family needs in order to be able to experience success. Aside from financial stability, she indicates that the following are all vital resources:

- Optimal health in the emotional, mental, spiritual, and physical realms.

- Adequate support systems involving appropriate relationships and role models.

- Some knowledge of "hidden rules," especially of the middle class, on which most schools base their educational approach.

Dr. Payne states, and CFK affirms, that "Resources of students and adults should be analyzed before dispensing advice or seeking solutions to situations … It costs nothing to be an appropriate role model." Productive listening on the part of professionals on the Team is one way to reactivate resources evident in the family's story—and to help establish resources still needed to effect positive change.

What might be in a Team Action Plan?

TRAVIS FAMILY

Mrs. Travis (not her real name) has five children. Three attend the elementary school that referred the family to CFK. Two children are in middle school; one of them was found by the schools to be mentally retarded and functioning on about the 5-year-old level, although he is now 13. In order to remove her children from the physical and emotional abuses of the father, Mrs. Travis is living in her station wagon with the children, sometimes at a local park. She moves her car periodically so that the father will not find them. She too has suffered many injuries at his hand. She doesn't want to press charges; she is clearly afraid. The children haven't been attending school on a regular basis, and the three in elementary school are not learning to the best of their abilities.

At our first CFK Team meeting, Mrs. Travis, with encouragement and help from the guidance counselor, told her story. At this time, all the other Team members made good use of their training in positive listening strategies. The mother revealed that she had held the same full-time job for ten years. This strength was noted in the minutes, as was her determination to protect her children. She reported leaving the children, when they weren't in school, in the McDonald's restaurant next to her workplace, with the middle school daughter in charge of keeping them safe. The mother said she leaves them there with a tote bag filled with markers, crayons, paper, coloring books, and crackers—and enough money for each to buy something to drink. Mrs. Travis demonstrated good planning skills as she spoke.

Although this mother had enough income to pay rent, she didn't have enough money accumulated to get a new place and pay two months' rent and a security deposit. It became clear that the mother and children needed counseling to counter the abuse they had experienced—to regain or recognize their own inner strengths. This family needed help with immediate and long-range planning. We started with an immediate Plan, upgrading it as progress allowed.

Mrs. Travis chose to receive domestic violence counseling and mentoring, as well as assistance with initiating divorce proceedings. The children made friends in the shelter housing as they participated in peer-group activities. The family was able to stay in a safe shelter program for two years while the mother received assistance building a "nest egg" and support to acquire independent housing. All of the children received play therapy and family therapy. They started attending school on a regular basis. During this transition it became apparent that two of the children were gifted, that one needed to continue in special education, and that the other two were fine average students who really enjoyed school. Mrs. Travis took a parenting class offered by the Cooperative Extension Office, enabling her to help the children catch up with schoolwork and adjust to their new lifestyle. She was able to continue in her job and to take advantage, for the first time, of her medical benefits. In addition, she joined a support group offered by the Association for Retarded Citizens and became more knowledgeable and adept at raising her older son. Mrs. Travis stated she was glad to have the two years the shelter placement offered and grateful that CFK gave her a chance to find herself: to stabilize her life and the lives of her children. New positive relationships were formed. Mrs. Travis developed close ties with the schools, and a new family emphasis on education was created. This particular CFK case was monitored by the Team for 27 months to a successful conclusion.

On the next page is an example of an Action Plan that would be applicable to the Travis case. Notice that there's a place on the form for the signatures and contact information of all present at the meeting. It also specifies who is responsible for supporting the parent at each step along the way. (You will find a blank form in the Appendix on page 70.)

Once formulated, copies of the Plan are given to all involved, a monitoring process begins, and the Plan is adjusted to meet ongoing needs.

Any Collaboration For Kids program has a CFK specialist as its coordinator. This can be the individual who first established the program or another visionary human services person dedicated to its goal. An optimal ratio seems to be one specialist for every eight elementary schools served. It's very important for the coordinating specialist to know and understand the workings of the school division and the individual schools in the program. It's also vital that this person have some background in social work, guidance counseling, or community resources. If the program is being initiated by an agency or individual, it's necessary to get the schools involved first. Chapter 7 of this book is a good reference for understanding just how the process moves along a continuum of action. There you'll find forms, memos, newsletters, letters of support, and other valuable information.

COLLABORATİON FOR KİDS TEAM ACTİON PLAN

Name _____ DOB _____

School _____ Date _____

Recommendations for Family	Facilitator Responsible	Expected Completion Date
Immediate safe shelter housing	Social Services Rep. / Parent	24 hours or sooner
Go to shelter housing with family	Social Services Rep.	24 hours or sooner
Children in school regularly	Guidance Counselor / Family	24 hours w/monitoring
After-school daycare	CFK Specialist	Two days
Implement safety pickup plan for school & daycare	Principal / Parent	Two days
Arrange bus transport from shelter	CFK Specialist	24 hours
Arrange counseling and play therapy	Mental Health Rep. / Parent	Two weeks
Mentoring for middle school child	Coop. Ext. Rep. / Parent	Two weeks
Tutor for elementary children	Principal / Teacher / Child	One week
Legal advice for mother	Court Services Rep. / Parent	Two weeks

Participants in plan development:

CFK specialist _____ Phone _____

Name _____ Position _____ Phone _____

Name _____ Position _____ Phone _____

Name _____ Position _____ Phone _____

Name _____ Position _____ Phone _____

Name _____ Position _____ Phone _____

Name _____ Position _____ Phone _____

Next meeting date _____ Time _____

Forward Actions

- Think of actual situations in your community that may have been improved by having this process in place. Document these situations for future use.

- Continue to expand your resource file (see Chapter 7).

- List principals and guidance counselors who might be interested in helping children in their schools by using this process.

- Identify an individual in the school division's Central Administration who would be willing to learn about this process from you.

- Prepare two or three reports of actual case-study families—whose identities must remain *anonymous*—for presentation to illustrate how CFK will work.

5

SETTING THE STAGE FOR A PILOT PROGRAM

A rock pile ceases to be a rock pile
the moment a single man contemplates it,
bearing within him the image of a cathedral.

—Antoine de Saint-Exupéry
French novelist

ENSURE THE AVAILABILITY OF YOUR STAKEHOLDERS

Before a single Team Plan can be implemented, Team players must be trained. And before a single training session can be scheduled, it's necessary to have met with, and have firmly on board, all the various stakeholders required for making this a truly collaborative journey.

To reiterate: First, this means that either the entire school division or at least a few elementary schools have committed to making a pilot program available to their children and families. (I found three schools to be an ideal number to start the program without overwhelming already stressed agencies.) Next, obtain from all relevant community agencies a commitment to participate. At this point, the commitment made is for participation in an initial pilot program; however, emphasize the real possibility of future growth due to success. Ask agencies and schools to commit staff personnel and adequate time for training and participation—probably one specific person per agency for up to one day a week at the beginning.

> **Start Small**
> **Stay Focused**
> **Be Prepared**

These representatives need to agree to be trained in the collaborative process and to implement it fully. All of the elements of collaboration (these were presented near the end of Chapter 2) are to be summarized, even though they won't necessarily be understood completely until the actual training takes place.

The following community agencies may be asked to participate in the pilot program:

- Schools
- Department of Social Services
- Department of Mental Health
- Court Services
- Cooperative Extension, if available
- Health Department, if applicable
- Others, as required

By this point, you will have a Team of about five committed individuals. The primary task of this small team is to build optimal working relationships by getting to know one another well, trusting in each person's desire to enhance the overall well-being of children. In addition, with a CFK specialist facilitating, these five individuals will begin the process of creating a glossary for what will become their common professional language. They'll agree on definitions for terms that will ultimately be used by all participants for communication during the collaborative process.

An agreement needs to be reached regarding common goals as the group works through the collaborative elements together. It's important to keep minutes of these discussions. Once this basic preliminary work is completed by the core group, a protocol for a CFK Team meeting, which will be conducted for each child referred, needs to be created. This will establish responsibilities for each professional before, during, and after the actual Team meetings. It's essential to agree on this protocol before communitywide training begins.

Here is the meeting protocol designed by the first pilot group in Prince William County, Virginia.

Responsibilities of School Representatives

Although normally several school staff members will participate on a given Team, each school is expected to have *one primary* contact person. Often the guidance counselor, school social worker, or assistant principal will fill this role.

Before the Meeting

- Explain to the parent(s) the CFK option and discuss the process of telling the family story.

- Complete the "universal" Consent to Release and Exchange Information form with the parent. This can be done with the assistance of the CFK specialists if a neutral party is needed (see Chapter 7).

- Complete and send the referral packet. This is to be done with input from the parent after examination of the Child Study Committee minutes.

- Notify the parent—in a supportive way—of meeting place and time, both in writing and by phone.

- Determine whether the parent needs transportation or childcare services in order to attend the meeting (that is, try to remove as many roadblocks as possible).

- For the meeting, secure a private room furnished with adult-size chairs and a writing table.

- Provide drinking water, pencils, paper, and a box of tissues.

- Notify participating school personnel of the meeting time and place. Provide a list to each prospective participant of exactly what is needed from him or her.

- Discuss with the child's teacher details of *what* will be reported at the meeting—and also *how*, emphasizing that the child's strengths will be presented first.

During the Meeting

- Be productive listeners; allow the parent to lead when possible.

- The teacher will report briefly on the student's strengths and the areas of concern in an objective way, avoiding the demonstration of negative emotions, such as frustration, irritation, or a feeling of futility. How to do this is part of the training (see Chapter 6).

- Other school staff will add to this report, if appropriate, offering support and reviewing past accommodations.

- Use the "co-investigation" approach (DeVol, 2004); see brief explanation at the end of this chapter.

- Be receptive to new information and suggestions. Participate with the parent in discussion and creation of "mental models" (word pictures or ways of visualizing the situation) that will ultimately shape the Team Action Plan.

- Each individual needs to be ready to implement his or her part of the Plan.

After the Meeting

- Continue to encourage the parent at the close of the meeting and over time.

- The school's main contact person must be available to answer any questions the parent may have about the Plan.

- Stay in contact with the CFK specialist regarding case progress— or lack thereof.

- Place the meeting room back in order, if necessary.

- Monitor and facilitate the school piece of the Team Action Plan.

Agency Representatives' Responsibilities

Before the Meeting

- Check the CFK calendar for meeting times, locations, and dates.

- Confirm meeting attendance.

- Provide a trained substitute if you must miss a meeting.

- Review intake data before the meeting.

During the Meeting

- Be prompt, attentive, and supportive.

- Use productive listening, and follow the "no lecturing" rule.

- Demonstrate respect and support for the parent and other Team members.

- Ask responsible questions.

- Help create mental models.

- Offer suggestions, services, support, and referrals during creation of the Team Action Plan.

- Claim your piece of the Plan.

- Communicate clearly.

After the Meeting

- Facilitate any pertinent Plan actions.

- Keep a record of communication with family, as well as actions taken.

- Maintain open communication with the CFK specialist regarding suggestions and progress—or lack thereof.

CFK Specialist's Responsibilities

Before the Meeting

- Staff the case with the school contact.

- Assist in explaining the program to the parent(s) and obtain his, her, or their signatures.

- Review referral information.

- Meet with the parent alone when appropriate.

- Place the meeting on the CFK calendar; notify all agencies involved.

- Confirm attendance and send out referral information for review.

- Arrive early at the school for the meeting.

- Bring Team Action Plan forms and other applicable materials.

During the Meeting

- As meeting facilitator, introduce all who are present (use name plates or stand-alone cards where each person is sitting).

- Set the stage for the meeting—statement of purpose and support, order of those speaking.

- Raise the parent's comfort level about being the primary Team member.

- Give an explanation of the meeting goal and the Team Action Plan.

- Encourage productive listening.

- Encourage parent expression, verbalization, and idea sharing.

- Keep the meeting moving in a positive direction; facilitate discussion.

- Write the Team Action Plan as it is created, listing each person's part.

- Clarify any questions. Reiterate the Team's support. Explain again how the Plan will unfold.

- Set a follow-up meeting date.

- Give the parent a copy of the Plan and contact information for all other Team members.

- Distribute copies of the Plan to all.

- Bring the meeting to a close.

- Encourage after-meeting conversations.

After the Meeting

- Facilitate participation by all and monitor progress.

- Maintain open communication by frequent contact with the parent, school, and agencies.

- Maintain an updated resources list.

- Maintain court/guardian *ad litem*/CASA (court-appointed special advocate) contact if appropriate.

- Maintain the case records overall.

- Maintain the statistics.

PARENT TEAM MEMBER RESPONSIBILITIES

- Share information with school and sign the permission form for CFK participation.

- Attend meetings; be on time.

- Share your family story with the Team.

- Express your perception of any issues or needs.

- Participate in discussion and the "co-investigation" process.

- Listen to others during discussion.

- Help create mental models applicable to your situation.

- Share in the creation of a Team Action Plan.

- Ask questions.

- Review and follow your Plan pieces.

- Be open to change.

- Suggest changes in the Plan that could be helpful to your family.

The reasons for creating a detailed protocol like this prior to training a larger group of participants is likely apparent by this point. Equipped with a common professional language and a meeting protocol, your core group is now ready to examine the process of training professionals from participating pilot schools and other community agencies.

FORWARD ACTIONS

- Review information discussed so far. Make a list of people you feel should be included in your CFK Pilot Program training session.

- As the CFK specialist, what content do you feel is pertinent to this training?

- List what you want to include in the training session, and then decide how long the session will last—one day, two days?

- Check any Central Office schedules for staff-development times; find some tentative dates.

- Meet again with your core group to plan the training session.

- Listen carefully to how core members envision the training.

- Discuss the creation and use of mental models.

- Gather available materials to teach productive listening (see end of next chapter for suggestions).

■   ■   ■

Co-investigation needs to involve the entire CFK team, with all recognizing the parent(s) as the most important Team member(s). Together, the Team begins the process of listening with new skills in place that allow the parent to tell the family story and lead the way to change.

Using Ruby Payne's *A Framework for Understanding Poverty* (Payne, 2005) for background and understanding (depending on the family situation, the book also contains information about hidden rules of middle class and wealth), the Team will ask questions and communicate supportively about those things that the parent wants to change. Internal and community resources will be identified, helping families become active problem solvers. With gentle guidance and mentoring, rather than delivering edicts and lecturing, co-investigation becomes the tool for change.

The parent is guided toward the following questions at the appropriate times:

1. Where am I now?

2. What are the causes?

3. Where does the power exist now?

4. Where do I want the power to be?

5. How do I shift the power?

6. How do I make change happen?

7. How do I recapture my own power?

8. What resources do I tap to regain my own power?

9. What is my responsibility in obtaining what is needed?

10. What are my intended results?

11. What do I want in the future?

Content and Tips:
Getting the Team Ready

*Spectacular achievements are always preceded
by unspectacular preparation.*

–Roger Staubach
Athlete and motivational speaker

The first CFK training session in Prince William County included a heavy dose of learning accompanied by an abundance of games, food, music, and inspirational sharing. The agenda was filled to capacity with vital information, and it moved quickly. Afterward, it was widely touted to have been the best staff development ever given in Prince William County. Everyone left with usable information; actual personal growth was evident everywhere. Letters and notes of appreciation arrived for weeks afterward.

The motto for that day was: "Let's talk about what we *can do* for children and families in this county and completely delete, for this day, things that we cannot do."

This set the appropriate mood.

At the beginning of the day, we asked all participants to write on a piece of paper all their doubts or negative feelings about the program's chances for success—or about just being at the staff development. We then had them ball this paper up, and we passed a trash can around for the purpose of collecting the negative feelings and attitudes. We left the trash can just outside the door and announced that if, at the end of the day, anyone still felt the need for those negative feelings or doubts, they could be retrieved on the way out. *No one stopped!*

The agenda for our first training day follows:

- Breakfast and welcome

- Housekeeping items: participants' folders, the day's schedule

- History of early intervention and overview of our common goal

- No Child Left Behind and other legislation

- The "unavailable to learn" child: the research and our role

- The idea, the purpose, the common language, the Team

- The parent as primary Team member, understanding the family story

- The job of the Team (individually and collectively)

- Productive listening as the key to communication

- Overview presentations by committed agencies regarding services and assistance available

- Team building and collaboration

- Working with school personnel toward success

- The role of the parent on the Team

- Choosing appropriate cases

- The referral process

- Obtaining parent permission, the "universal" Consent to Release and Exchange Information form

- What to expect at a meeting

- Role plays regarding meetings

- Forms, process, follow-through, scheduling meetings, record keeping

- Confidentiality

- Open communication

- Networking

It's important that all trainees understand the special education process in the participating school division. CFK programs *are not special education-specific.* CFK programs are for all children, *including* those in special education. It's also important to point out that this program is *not intended to be primarily for crisis intervention in true emergency (that is, immediately life-threatening) situations* but that resources for such occurrences will be provided.

TIPS FOR INITIAL TRAINING

It soon became clear that although this day was hugely successful, there hadn't been enough time to really teach everything. The following year we added much more collaboration training and several more activities by expanding into an additional half-day. A day and a half proved to be just right. During the original one-day training session we used music at several junctures: upon entering in the morning, at breaks, after lunch, and to close at the end of the day. We had made an "overview" video of the program that proved to be a good opener in the morning, explaining what we were about to accomplish; this also had been useful in many other settings. We hung banners and posters of positive quotes and sayings around the room; these became very popular with the participants and continue to be used in our program. (Some examples are provided in Chapter 7, as well as the start of each chapter of this book.) We handed out donated prizes to break up the day and lighten the mood. We provided baskets of "Life Savers" on each table for enjoyment when a boost was needed, and cold drinking water was always available. The trainees clearly appreciated these small touches.

SOME POSITIVE MUSIC

"Let There Be Peace on Earth"

"The Greatest Love of All"

"You Raise Me Up"

"Teach Your Children Well"

Peace Is the World Smiling, CD
From "Music for Little People"
P.O. Box 1460
Redway, CA 95560

SUMMARY OF TIPS

Allow a day and a half for training.

Focus on collaboration activities and training, as well as on teaching productive listening skills.

Every stakeholder agency makes a presentation.

Use music.

Use PowerPoint.

Leave time for personal networking.

Decorate with posters of positive quotes and sayings.

Keep water and snacks available.

Give prizes at odd times throughout the day.

Now that we've presented an overview of the training, let's look at some of the details. We used a great deal of the training time to focus on all of the committed agencies and their functions, as well as the schools involved. Extending the session to a day and a half left plenty of time for addressing questions, which immediately created more positive relationships among future Team representatives. Overall, school staff members learned more about the wealth of services available through the agencies, and agency personnel were made more aware of the efforts undertaken by schools prior to making a call for help. This exchange resulted in excellent sharing of ideas, even a sense of rising hope in the room.

We were then ready to discuss how collaboration really works. We used the following resource materials:

- Two books by H.G. Garner: *Helping Others Through Teamwork* (2000) and *Teamwork Models and Experience in Education* (1995)

- D.C. Fogg's *Team-Based Strategic Planning* (1994)

- G.I. Maerhoff's *Team Building for School Change* (1993)

- Mattessich and Monsey's *Collaboration: What Makes It Work— A Review of the Research Literature Describing Factors Which Influence the Success of Collaboration* (1992)

- Some material from my own doctoral dissertation: *Children Unavailable: A Critical Analysis of Collaboration Between School Professionals and Child Protective Services in Issues of Child Abuse and Neglect* (1998)

We were now armed and ready to teach this not-so-natural process.

TIPS FOR TEACHING

1. Review and reaffirm the common goal.

2. Agree on shared leadership and responsibility.

3. Discuss the Team process that involves personal interaction, clear and frequent communication, productive listening, trust building, creative problem solving, individual accountability, conflict management, and development of interpersonal skills.

4. Clarify meeting rules and procedures.

5. Use Garner's *Helping Others Through Teamwork* to educate about:

   a. *Joining:* Building relationships, developing trust and openness, developing Team identity and loyalty

   b. *Storming:* A stage when differences of values and style emerge, when there's competition among members, and when conflicts arise

   c. *Norming:* Building team values and expectations, team rituals and traditions, and shared leadership

   d. *Performing:* Task focus, mutual support and feedback, flexibility, and role release

6. When planning the session, actively use the information on collaboration presented in Chapter 2 to create activities, materials, and discussions.

7. Within reason, learn as much as possible about your participants when planning to train.

Collaboration is crucial for Team participation. If we are to collaborate, we must understand who we're doing this for, why we're doing it, and how our roles interrelate. We know that efforts in the past made by agencies and schools working in isolation often haven't worked optimally for children and their families. The most effective training sessions focus on how collaborative efforts can work *from now on.* Use the research and statistics presented in Chapter 1 to emphasize the need for a collaborative program like this.

PRODUCTIVE LISTENING

A vital piece of training is teaching knowledgeable professionals how to listen productively. As professionals, most of us are very used to problem solving and telling others what to do. CFK promotes *learning FOR all through listening BY all.* It's of utmost importance to listen to the parent tell the family story—and to understand that perspective—in order to provide non-critical assistance toward the goal of assuming a leadership role for change in the family. Using productive listening, we can help parents create mental models to assist in sequencing, identifying family resources, exploring options, and gathering support for change (DeVol, 2004). Using productive listening, we demonstrate respect for the family, actively acknowledge the issues to be changed, and affirm the parent's leadership role on the Team.

Training professionals in the art of productive listening may require both practice and patience. It isn't necessarily easy to make the switch from lecturer to listener!

The productive listener will:

- Listen with a respectful and open mind.

- Listen to the voice and to the manner in which the story is told.

- Take notes and sequence.

- Listen to, and make a note of, parental strengths and resources.

- Listen for possible ideas for mental models.

- Avoid using what is shared by others largely as a springboard for telling one's *own* stories and anecdotes, no matter how closely related. A little of this can be empathetic, even compassionate, while a lot of this defeats the purpose of productive listening.

- Note ideas and questions for further discussion.

Ruby Payne's *A Framework for Understanding Poverty* and Philip DeVol's *Getting Ahead in a Just-Gettin'-By World* are useful resources for understanding productive listening. Another resource worth its weight in gold is *Bridges Out of Poverty* by Payne, DeVol, and Terie Dreussi Smith. Although we won't deal exclusively with individuals in economic poverty on our Teams, many concepts useful for finding one's way out of poverty are applicable to solving other problems as well. As noted earlier, Dr. Payne's work also imparts an understanding of the hidden rules of poverty, middle class, and wealth.

Four other useful resources on listening are *The Accidental Manager* by Gary Topchik (2003); www.kidsource.com, where you'll find "How Can Parents Model Good Listening Skills" by Carl Smith; www.infoplease.com (Listening Skills); and the Student Handbook: Listening Skills at www.d.umn.edu.

Forward Actions

- Gather as many local statistics as possible to support your program.

- Decide how to utilize the "red flag" behaviors presented in Chapter 3 in your efforts to help others realize the need for taking collaborative action in your community.

■ Plan to utilize descriptions of these "red flag" behaviors in training sessions to help others recognize the child who is "unavailable to learn."

■ Review and discuss various productive-listening training materials.

Taking Action:
Practical Help for Gathering Resources

An ounce of action is worth a ton of theory.

–Friedrich Engels
German philosopher and writer

In this chapter you'll find sample documents and other materials that may prove useful when starting your own Collaboration For Kids program. Regional differences will need to be taken into account when compiling your glossary of common language, and you'll likely use a somewhat different list of agencies. CFK's success in Prince William County is partly due to the extensive research done initially for assembly of an exhaustive list of county and state services, plus the care given to documentation during the program's establishment. Use the following pages as a guide to create your own materials—or download forms from the CD provided with this book (a listing of what appears on the CD can be found immediately after the Epilogue).

The first group of documents creates a good introductory packet of information that can be used to present the CFK concept to other professionals and to demonstrate its success. You will find:

1. Two pages of facts from the Prince William County program.

2. A year-by-year report demonstrating how one program progressed.

Also found in this chapter are a variety of other useful forms and lists of suggestions. Available in the Appendix is further information and documentation that will help you move forward with your own program.

Introduction to Collaboration for Kids

What Is It?

- An early-intervention, prevention, diversion, regular education process for preschool and elementary school children who are "unavailable to learn" due to problems outside of school.

- A collaborative effort to prevent further escalation of documented difficulties and future legal involvement.

- An effort to stabilize the family and help the child become a successful learner.

- An effort to rule in or out a child's need for special education services.

- An effort to reduce future court involvement.

- An effort to ensure a safer, healthier community.

The CFK program is implemented through meetings in the school with the parent(s), a CFK facilitator, and appropriate community agency representatives. These meetings are intended to provide support for parental leadership in planning for change and success.

Who Is the 'Unavailable to Learn' Child?

The "unavailable to learn" child is the one who, due to difficulties outside of school, is not learning successfully. The child is identified by school professionals as one who needs more help than normal academic accommodation and assistance provide—and who is demonstrating one or more symptoms on the "red flag" behaviors list (see page 19).

Who Are the Anticipated Collaborators?

The collaborators are the parent(s); a school administrator; the teacher; the school social worker and/or psychologist; the guidance counselor; and trained Team members from Child Protective Services, mental health, court services, and other agencies, as needed (substance abuse counselor, domestic violence counselor, public health nurse, parenting instructor, family physician, police, Cooperative Extension Program).

What About Confidentiality?

A "universal" Consent to Release and Exchange Information form, approved by legal counsel for all participating agencies, is signed by the parent(s) prior to the first meeting. This permits more open communication among Team members, including the parent(s), greatly increasing the likelihood of success.

What Is the Goal of Collaboration For Kids?

The goal of CFK is prevention, early intervention, and diversion on the preschool and elementary levels. The CFK Team will actively maximize assistance given to the child and family through a Team Action Plan to provide appropriate support, services, referrals, and resources. This results in more efficient and cost-effective use of services available in the community at large. Another goal of CFK is to maximize positive parental participation by supporting parents' inner strengths and restoring confidence in their ability to successfully access outer resources. Through this process, the ultimate goal of CFK is family stabilization for the well-being of the child—to ensure that the rights of education, safety, nurturance, and optimal physical and emotional health are realized.

What Are the Proven Results?

- Reduced truancy and tardiness

- Increased parental participation, responsibility, and guided follow-through

- Improved academic progress

- Fewer classroom disruptions

- Increased teaching time

- Improved behavior

- Reduced number of referrals to special education

- More appropriate and facilitated use of community services

- Reduced recidivism rate of cases

- Probable reduction of numbers of middle and high school students in court system

- Stabilized children and families

- Safer communities

COMPREHENSIVE CHILD STUDY YEAR-TO-YEAR REPORT

	1998–1999	1999–2000	2000–2001	2001–2002	2002–2003	2003–2004	2004–2005
Number of schools	3	10	24	24	37	39	44
Number of cases	14	50	121	122	152	209*	
Consults						62	
Number of cases with forward progress** in at least one area of concern	14	45	115	119	126	180	
Number of children and siblings served by CCS	39	106	262	310	314	438	
Number of classmates impacted***	97	265	655	775	785	1095	
Total number of children impacted	136	371	917	1085	1099	1533	

Intake Issues

Children usually come to intake with more than one of the following problems:

23% Child protection

11% Domestic violence

71% Mental health

28% Basic needs

32% Truancy/tardiness

61% Academic/IEP (individualized education plan)

26% Medical

59% Parent participation (in children's issues)

41% Parent compliance (with school community regulations, laws, and plans)

18% Other (traumatic incident, parental substance abuse, prison, parent court involvement, etc.)

Case Progress

89.1% Improvement in one or more areas

---

* 202 active cases, with 7 monitored

** Forward progress was measured by improved academic performance, increased parental participation, improved behavior, improved attendance, and referrals to and participation with appropriate community agencies. Cases often had more than one area of concern.

*** Impact on classmates was calculated using number of impacted children × 2.5.

INSPIRATIONAL QUOTATIONS

Here are some inspirational quotations we used on posters during our training sessions. Most of these don't have a documented source because they were taken from a convention button, a bumper sticker, another poster, or are just something said by a friend. We thank the authors, known and unknown. We're grateful to the unrecognized originators of the wisdom offered below. We're glad they can inspire us to do our best for children.

- The future depends on what we do in the present!

- Our children are living messages we send into a time and place we will never see.

- It is easier to build a child than repair an adult.

- The greatest natural resource any country can have is its children.

- Children are fragile; handle with care.

- "If we are to reach real peace in the world, we shall have to begin with the children."   –Mohandas K. Gandhi

- "It has become appallingly clear that our technology has surpassed our humanity."   –Albert Einstein

- Blessed are the flexible, for they shall not be bent out of shape.

- Life's important challenges all come down to the decision to get on with it, the courage to hold on, and the willingness to pedal like crazy.

- Character has no color. Integrity has no age. Honesty has no gender. Compassion has no height or weight. Caring has no language. Connecting has no handicap. Relationships have no degrees or certificates.

The following is a sample glossary of common professional language used to support and enhance our CFK Team communication. Establishing a glossary gives all Team members a better understanding of each stakeholder agency or profession involved. Having this glossary greatly facilitates Team communication and helps prevent misunderstandings.

Create your own glossary, with the input of all stakeholders, during one of the first organizational meetings.

The glossary will begin with foundational terms and input. As time goes on, it will grow because of ongoing input by stakeholders, and it will change because of the transient nature of policies and guidelines.

Establish a common language ...

SAMPLE

GLOSSARY OF TERMS

AEP: Alternative education plan is an individualized education plan for a student who is not receiving special education but who requires individualized attention to achieve academically. This plan shall address, but not be limited to, the following: academic performance level; learning style; career inventory information; documentation of guidance counseling, goals and expectations, and alternate placement.

CAEA: Court-appointed education advocates are volunteers who maintain two hours a week of contact with truant students to monitor attendance and to provide support and, possibly, tutoring.

CASA: Court-appointed special advocates are trained volunteers who act as the court's eyes and ears for child abuse and neglect cases.

CSC: Child Study Committee is the school's regular education process that establishes discussions between school professionals and parents of students who are having difficulty in school for any reason. Accommodations to remediate any difficulties are put into place through this committee. It's also the committee that will make referrals to Collaboration For Kids.

CHIN/SU: Child in need of supervision is a petition filed with the court to direct the appropriate public agencies to evaluate a child's service needs using an interdisciplinary team approach. The child or parent may be ordered to participate in treatment programs or services and to meet certain obligations.

Collaboration: Working together with a common goal and a shared responsibility for achieving that goal; working together with mutual respect, equality, and open, positive communication; using a common language for the benefit of the child and family.

CPS: Child Protective Services (a part of the Department of Social Services).

CSB: Community Services Board (mental health, substance abuse, mental retardation, prevention services, emergency services, parent/infant information).

CSU: Court Services Unit (juvenile probation, court intake, court counseling).

Diversion: To prevent court action; to prevent establishment of a court record.

Early intervention: For CFK, this refers to action taken early in life, not necessarily early in the difficulty; so action taken on behalf of a child who is between preschool age and Grade 5 in order to remediate situations both inside and outside of school that are rendering a child "unavailable to learn." The focus is on the child, and the family also will benefit.

Below is a list of other terms you might want to define for your collaborative purposes.

ADDITIONAL TERMS TO CONSIDER

Founded

Unfounded

Mandated reporter

Prevention

Truancy

Tardiness

Interdiction

Excused absence

Unexcused absence

Multidisciplinary team (MDT)

Individuals with Disabilities Education Act (IDEA)

Special education

Eligibility

Individualized education plan (IEP)

Functional behavior assessment (FBA)

Other special education terms commonly used in your schools

Other legal terms commonly used in your area's court system

There's a multitude of services that every jurisdiction offers its population. Useful examples and areas to explore are listed here. When gathering community and state data, include as many of the following areas as possible:

Nutrition

Pregnancy

Medicaid-related services

Medical referral and support

Free clinics

Medical transport

Prescription assistance programs

Vision and hearing programs

Speech and language programs

Medicaid optometrists

Dental help

AIDS programs

Mentor programs and resources

Support groups and resources

Childcare options

Emergency assistance resources

Housing and shelters

Domestic violence assistance

Transitional housing

Sexual assault assistance

Seniors' housing

Child abuse and neglect assistance

Financial assistance

Parenting program

Tutoring

Summer programs

Court and legal services

Leisure and recreation options

Adult education/GED (general educational development) resources

Special education resources outside of school

Counseling resources with or without Medicaid

Psychiatric hospitals, treatment centers, clinics

COLLABORATION FOR KIDS REFERRAL PACKET

The forms shown on the following pages are included in the referral packet we use. This is updated and sent to participating schools every year. The trained school contact person will know how to use these forms and will review the referral process with school staff. Included in our packet are:

- Program explanation reminder

- Explanation of the referral process

- "Universal" Consent to Release and Exchange Information form in English and Spanish

- Case referral profile

- Student assistance checklist

- List of emergency resources

PROGRAM EXPLANATION

Collaboration For Kids (CFK) is an early-intervention program for children in preschool through Grade 5 who are experiencing academic difficulty due to factors occurring outside of the school or learning environment. This program allows parents to collaborate with representatives from the school and community agencies serving children and their families. It's a process of intervention and stabilization through community collaboration.

Our goals are to remove barriers to a child's ability to learn and to improve the overall well-being of the child. The problems impacting children referred to CFK have frequently been long-standing, if not generational. CFK is not a quick fix. It's possible that the program's Team will work with and/or follow a child and family for months, if not years. The earlier we can intervene in a child's life and in the identified problem, the better the prognosis for change. CFK specialists are available to discuss potential referrals, so please don't spend time wondering whether you should call for more information. Call—and together a decision can be made regarding options.

Collaboration For Kids *is not primarily an emergency intervention program.* We have found that the most common requests for emergency needs are for food, shelter, medical help, and child and adult protective assistance. Here is a list of community agencies having resources to meet those types of sudden emergencies.

_____

_____

_____

_____

_____

SAMPLE

Collaboration For Kids Referral Process

Referring a student to Collaboration For Kids (CFK) involves the following steps:

Step 1: A Child Study Committee* meeting is conducted to discuss a student's school difficulties with the parent. During this process it may be noted that there are issues outside of the school environment that are interfering with a student's ability to learn.

Step 2: The school's Child Study Committee identifies and implements strategies to address these outside issues, documenting discussions in CSC minutes and the Child Study Plan.

Step 3: The Child Study Committee evaluates the success of the attempted strategies and discusses the appropriateness of a referral to CFK. Once the decision is made to refer, the Child Study Committee appoints a contact person to work with the parent and the CFK specialist. The contact person is responsible for reviewing case information with the CFK specialist.

NOTE: If a child has been in Child Study for a while, and documentation reflects attempted interventions, Steps 1–3 may be collapsed. If the parent is present and interested in CFK, a consent form can be signed at the meeting, but see Step 4: Make sure the parent understands what the consent means.

Step 4: The school contact person discusses CFK with the parent and completes the consent form.

NOTE: A signed CFK consent does not always mean that a full CFK meeting will be take place. In some cases the needed resources can be identified and accessed without a meeting. It's prudent to explain to the parent that the consent form and the referral packet are the vehicle within the school system used to explore the possibility of obtaining additional community resources.

* The parent is a member of the Child Study Committee.

Step 5: The school contact person completes the two-page CFK referral/profile form. The school sends the completed form and required school information to the CFK specialist.

Step 6: Upon receipt of a completed packet, the CFK specialist contacts the school representative to discuss the case. As a result of the discussion, either of the following may occur:

1. The CFK specialist may provide some referrals to the school representative without having a CFK meeting.

2. A CFK meeting may be scheduled with appropriate community representatives.

NOTE: A CFK meeting will not be scheduled prior to the receipt, from the school, of a completed packet that must include:

- Minutes from the last two Child Study meetings, including Teacher Education Reports

- A copy of the report card and other documentation showing academic difficulty

- Discipline and attendance records, if applicable

- A signed CFK consent form

SAMPLE

COLLABORATION FOR KIDS CASE REFERRAL/PROFILE
_____ SCHOOL DIVISION

Student _____   Student # _____

DOB _____   CA _____   Race _____

School _____   Grade _____   Teacher _____

Special Education? ❏ yes ❏ no   Disability Label _____

Name of parents _____

Address _____   Phone _____

Siblings:

Name _____   School _____   Age _____

Name _____   School _____   Age _____

Health coverage? ❏ yes ❏ no

If there is no health insurance, refer to _____

Medicaid? ❏ yes ❏ no

Private health insurance _____

Name of provider _____

Pertinent information (family dynamics, current services and provider, ESOL, LEP, etc.)

_____

_____

Presenting concerns and background (use Parent Information, Child Study Minutes)

_____

_____

Recommendations and accommodations made to date with results

_____

_____

Referral date to CFK _____   Date consent form signed _____

Desired outcomes of CFK _____

_____

_____

STUDENT ASSISTANCE REQUIREMENTS: A CHECKLIST

SAMPLE

Student _____   Date _____

DOB _____   Grade _____

❑ Academic failure
❑ Frequent absences
❑ Frequent tardiness
❑ School avoidance
❑ Multiple discipline referrals
    ❑ Multiple suspensions
    ❑ Long-term suspension
    ❑ Threat assessment (in progress or completed)
❑ Poor hygiene
❑ Disruptive
❑ Non-compliant
❑ Basic resources (housing, food, clothing)
❑ Family and/or student illness
❑ Substance abuse
❑ Domestic violence
❑ Neglect
❑ Supervision issues
❑ Poor communication
❑ Previous Family Assessment and Planning Team (FAPT) involvement
❑ Custody or dispute issues

❑ Fighting
❑ Cruelty toward others/animals
❑ Abusive (threatening, uses force)
❑ Inappropriate sexual knowledge
❑ Isolated
❑ Limited social skills
❑ Withdrawn
❑ Anxious/worried
❑ Depressed
❑ Emotional blunting
❑ Sleep disturbances
❑ Eating concerns
❑ Mental health involvement
❑ Suicidal threats/ideation
❑ Has made suicide attempt
❑ Social services involvement
❑ Foster care
❑ Vandalism
❑ Fire setting
❑ Involvement in legal system
❑ Runaway behavior
❑ Theft

Additional information related to above concerns: _____

_____

_____

_____

Person completing the form: _____

SAMPLE

CONSENT TO RELEASE AND EXCHANGE INFORMATION

I understand that different agencies provide different services and benefits. Each agency must have specific information in order to provide these services and benefits. By signing this form, I am allowing agencies to exchange certain information so it will be easier for them to work together effectively to provide or coordinate these services or benefits.

I, _____, am signing this form for
(Full printed name of consenting person or persons)

_____
(Full printed name of client)

_____
(Client's Address)

_____   _____
(Client's date of birth)   (Client's SSN—optional)

My relationship to the client is: ❑ Self   ❑ Parent   ❑ Guardian

I want the following confidential information about the client (except drug or alcohol abuse diagnoses and treatment) to be exchanged:

❑ Yes	❑ No	Assessment information	❑ Yes	❑ No	Medical diagnosis
❑ Yes	❑ No	Educational records	❑ Yes	❑ No	Financial information
❑ Yes	❑ No	Mental health diagnosis	❑ Yes	❑ No	Psychiatric records
❑ Yes	❑ No	Benefits/services needed, planned, and/or received	❑ Yes	❑ No	Medical records
			❑ Yes	❑ No	Criminal justice records
❑ Yes	❑ No	Psychological records	❑ Yes	❑ No	Employment records

Other Information (write in): _____

I want (name of school division): _____
(Name and address of referring agency and staff contact person)

and the following other agencies to be able to exchange this information:

❑ County Mental Health Agency   ❑ Court Services Unit   ❑ Other _____
❑ County Department of Social Services   ❑ Cooperative Extension   ❑ Other _____

I want this information to be exchanged ONLY for the following purpose(s):
❑ Service coordination and treatment planning
❑ Other _____

I want information to be shared (check all that apply):
❑ In writing   ❑ In meetings or by phone   ❑ Computerized data

I want to share additional information received after this consent is signed: ❑ Yes   ❑ No

This consent is good until (date) _____

■ I can withdraw this consent at any time by telling the referring agency. This will stop the listed agencies from sharing information after they know my consent has been withdrawn. I have the right to know what information about me has been shared—and why, when, and with whom it was shared. If I ask, each agency will show me this information.

■ I want all the agencies to accept a copy of this form as a valid consent to share information.

■ If I do not sign this form, information will not be shared, and I will have to contact each agency individually to give them information about me that they need.

Signature(s) _____   Date _____
(Consenting person or persons)

Person Explaining Form _____
                          (Name)   (Title)   (Phone)

Witness (if required) _____
                       (Signature)   (Address)   (Phone)

Permiso Para Intercambiar Información

SAMPLE

Yo entiendo que diferentes agencies proporcionan diferentes servicios y beneficios. Cada agencia tiene que tener información especifica para poder proporcionar servicios y beneficios. Al firmar este documento yo estoy permitiendo a las agencias intercambiar cierta información para que sea más fácil para ellos trabajar eficazmente para proveer y coordinar estos servicios y beneficios.

Yo, _____ , estoy firmando este documento por
(ESCRIBE EL NOMBRE COMPLETO DE LA PERSONA / PERSONAS QUE ESTA/N DANDO CONSENTIMIENTO)

_____
(ESCRIBE EN LETRA DE MOLDE EL NOMBRE COMPLETO DEL CLIENTE)

_____
(DIRECCION DEL CLIENTE)

_____   _____
(FECHA DE NACIMIENTO DEL CLIENTE)   (NUMERO DEL SS OPCIONAL)

Mi relación con el cliente es:
❑ Propia   ❑ Padre   ❑ Poder de Abogado   ❑ Guardian   ❑ Otro Representante Legal Autorizado

Yo quiero la siguiente información confidencial acerca del cliente (con excepción del diagnostico de abuso o tratamiento de drogas o alcohol) que sea intercambiada:

Sí No		Sí No		Sí No	
❑ ❑	Información de Asesoramiento	❑ ❑	Diagnostico Medico	❑ ❑	Records de Educación
❑ ❑	Información Financiera	❑ ❑	Diagnostico de Salud Mental	❑ ❑	Records Psiquiátricos
❑ ❑	Beneficios/Servicios Necesitados Planeados, y/o Recibidos	❑ ❑	Records Médicos	❑ ❑	Records de Justicia Criminal
		❑ ❑	Records Psicológicos	❑ ❑	Records de Empleo

Otra información (escriba) _____
Yo quiero _____

(NOMBRE Y DIRECCIÓN DE LA AGENCIA Y DE UNA PERSONA DE CONTACTO DE PERSONAL)
Y las siguientes agencias que puedan intercambiar esta información:
❑ County Mental Health Agency   ❑ Court Services Unit   ❑ Other _____
❑ County Department of Social Services   ❑ Cooperative Extension   ❑ Other _____

Yo quiero que esta información sea cambiada SOLAMENTE por él (los) siguiente(s) propósito(s):
❑ Coordinación de Servicios y Planeamiento de Tratamiento   ❑ Determinación de Elegibilidad
Otra (escriba) _____
Yo quiero que la información sea compartida (marque todos los que aplican):
❑ Información por Escrito   ❑ En Reunión o Por teléfono   ❑ Datos Computarizados
Yo quiero compartir información adicional recibida después que este consentimiento sea firmado: ❑ Sí ❑ No
Este consentimiento es bueno hasta él: _____
Yo puedo retirar este consentimiento a cualquier hora llamando a la oficina de referencia. Esto impediría que las agencias compartieran información después que ellos se enteren que mi consentimiento ha sido cancelado. Yo tengo el derecho de conocer la información que ha sido compartida acerca de mi persona, y porque, cuando, y con quien ha sido compartido. Si yo pregunto, cada agencia me enseñara la información. Yo quiero que todas estas agencias acepten una copia de esta forma como un consentimiento valido para compartir información.
Si yo no firmo esta forma, información no podrá ser compartida y yo tendré que comunicarme con cada agencia individualmente para darles la información mía que ellos necesiten.

Firma(s) _____   Fecha _____
(PERSONA O PERSONAS QUE DAN CONSENTIMIENTO)
Persona Explicando la Forma _____
(Nombre)   (Título)   (Número de Teléfono)
Testigo (sí es requerido) _____
(Nombre)   (Dirección)   (Número de Teléfono)

SAMPLE

Resources

Emergency Needs

Name of homeless shelter *Phone #* For financial help must have cutoff notice	**Salvation Army** *Phone #* Food and financial assistance
Department of Social Services *Services and phone #*	**Catholic Charities** *phone #* Food, clothing, referrals, rent and utilities (when funds are available)
Food Closet and Emergency Assistance *Phone #*	**St. Vincent DePaul** *phone #* Emergency financial assistance

Housing/Shelters
Names and phone numbers of all local shelters and housing programs

Health Care
Names and contacts for all healthcare and free clinic programs, medical transport, and emergency medical assistance
Phone #'s

Domestic Violence
Emergency counseling centers, hotlines, and shelters with phone numbers

----

Suspect Child Abuse/Neglect?

State and local Child Protection phone numbers for reporting purposes

Child Supervision Guidelines for Your Jurisdiction

Before being left alone, children need to be trained in self-care techniques, such as knowledge of how to deal with: emergencies, conflicts with friends/siblings, handling loneliness/boredom, personal safety, simple first aid, and fear. They must know how to reach a responsible adult if needed.

General Guidelines for the State of Virginia

Child Supervision	Childcare Guidelines
0–8 May not be left unsupervised	12–13 May baby-sit children up to four hours
9–11 No more than 1.5 hours alone—days only	14–15 May baby-sit over four hours—not overnight or over weekends
12–15 May be left alone all day	16–17 May baby-sit children over night or over weekends
16–17 May be left alone all night or over weekends	

For additional resource information, contact your Collaboration For Kids specialist.

COLLABORATION FOR KIDS
TEAM ACTION PLAN

The form on the next page is used with the parent(s) during collaborative Team meetings. It's used to show, in concrete form, all the supports, resources, and services that are to be put into place for the child and family. All appropriate contact information is written on the Plan, including a phone number for each Team member. As the parent becomes active as the leader of the Action Plan, much support is given by other Team members. Each Team member accepts a piece of the Plan, and each receives a copy.

At this point, monitoring begins as the parent receives help and nurturance while accomplishing the steps in the Plan, one at a time. Clearly the Plan must deal with the most important issues first. The Plan changes and evolves, as needed, and as progress is made.

| SAMPLE | COLLABORATION FOR KIDS TEAM ACTION PLAN |

Name _____ DOB _____

School _____ Date _____

Recommendations for Family	Facilitator Responsible	Expected Completion Date

Participants in plan development:

CFK specialist _____ Phone _____

Name _____ Position _____ Phone _____

Name _____ Position _____ Phone _____

Name _____ Position _____ Phone _____

Name _____ Position _____ Phone _____

Name _____ Position _____ Phone _____

Name _____ Position _____ Phone _____

Next meeting date _____ Time _____

Parent and Stakeholder Surveys

Participation and positive communication by parents are keys to successful problem solving when working toward solutions for children. How parents feel about their CFK experience is important, and we frequently request feedback.

On the following page is a parent survey form that will be useful for recording reactions and suggestions for program growth and development, as well as information you'll need to maintain statistics. If you have sufficient communication with the parent and have offered the ongoing support needed, you'll be pleased with the feedback you receive. We've found it useful to meet with the parent to discuss responses on the form, as this enhances our understanding of reactions, ultimately helping us do the best job possible for all concerned.

The stakeholder survey records feedback and suggestions from agency professionals on the CFK Teams. Using this has provided us with remarkable insights and many creative ideas.

HINT: Complex forms result in NO response. Keep these forms simple!

COLLABORATION FOR KIDS
PARENT STAKEHOLDER SURVEY FORM

Please complete the following brief survey. Feel free to comment in the section provided. On a scale of 1 (poor) to 10 (outstanding), please rate the following:

_____ 1. The Collaboration For Kids program has helped my child and family.

_____ 2. The Team members have been supportive and helpful.

_____ 3. I have been able to make adequate phone or e-mail contact with needed resource people.

_____ 4. I feel we have made progress through this program.

_____ 5. The recommended resources and services have been helpful.

_____ 6. Overall communication with the Team has worked well.

_____ 7. My role as a Team participant has been positive.

_____ 8. Team members listened well and heard what I had to say.

Comments:

_____

_____

_____

COLLABORATION FOR KIDS
AGENCY/SCHOOL STAKEHOLDER QUESTIONNAIRE

Please respond to the following three questions. Your input into the CFK process is very important; it helps us maintain a healthy program.

_____ 1. How would you rate the overall CFK program—on a scale of 1 (ineffective) to 10 (very effective)? Please comment on what you feel has worked well and what you feel needs improvement.

_____

_____

_____

_____ 2. How would you rate follow-up and communication between/among agencies—on a scale of 1 to 10? Please comment on strengths or weaknesses.

_____

_____

_____

_____ 3. How would you rate the current collaborative efforts between agencies—on the same 1 to 10 scale? Comments and suggestions welcome.

_____

_____

_____

Please use the back of this questionnaire to give further feedback.

Name _____

Agency _____   Date _____

KIDS COUNT

KEEPING STATISTICS

The charts that follow illustrate the areas in which we maintain statistics. During the pilot program, everything was done by the CFK specialist. Now, however, due to the large size of the Prince William County program, data are gathered by the CFK specialists, then are sent to the school division's Office of Planning and Assessment where statistics are generated. These statistics are presented regularly to the school board, agency directors, judges, and, of course, participating Team members. This is why it's vitally important to document, document, document. It's exciting to see the figures emerge over time.

COLLABORATION FOR KIDS
SAMPLE DATA SHEET*

Student status					
Participating (N = 202)			Observation (N = 69)		Total
Active	Moved	Closed	Monitor	Consult	
107	38	57	7	62	271

Participating	Percentage
Special education	46.0%
Regular education	54.0%
Minority	45.5%
LEP	5.4%
Free/reduced-price lunch	58.4%

* Data report includes students on active, moved, or closed status (participating) with activity during reporting period. Data report does not include students on monitor or consult status (observation).

Students making progress in at least one area of concern		
Number participating	Number improved	Percentage improved
202	180	89.1%

Total number impacted	
Number of children impacted, including siblings	438
Number of children impacted, including classmates*	1,095
Total number of children impacted	1,533

Concerns	Number presenting	Percentage of participating students	Improved	
			N	%
Truant / tardy	64	31.7%	45	70.3%
Academic / IEP	124	61.4%	83	66.9%
Behavior	154	75.2%	106	69.7%
Medical	53	26.2%	37	69.8%

Family issues	Number presenting	Percentage of participating students	Improved	
			N	%
Child protection	47	23.3%	35	74.5%
Domestic violence	22	10.9%	12	54.5%
Mental health	144	71.3%	104	72.2%
Basic needs	56	27.7%	38	67.9%
Parent participation	119	58.9%	85	71.4%
Parent compliance	82	40.6%	54	65.9%
Other	36	17.8%	24	66.7%

* Impact on classmates was calculated using number of children impacted × 2.5.

FORWARD ACTIONS

- Begin to construct a glossary of terms common to your areas of expertise, using clear definitions.

- In studying the forms in this chapter, where would you need to make alterations to fit your envisioned program?

- Complete a resources page similar to page 68, using the appropriate resource information in your community.

In Conclusion, Let's Begin!

*Don't be afraid to go out on a limb,
for that is where the fruit is.*

–Author unknown

Education is all a matter of building bridges.

–Ralph Ellison
U.S. essayist and novelist

Today, as I write this book, I received a phone call from the supervisor of the Prince William County CFK (CCS) initiative. I sit in amazement at my desk as she relates the gratifying good news. The superintendent of Prince William County Schools has mandated that *all* the division's elementary schools (55 in 2005–06) must participate in this dynamic initiative—and that the program itself will become a permanent fixture in the budget beginning the following year.

Collaboration For Kids began as an outgrowth of my doctoral dissertation in the three elementary schools I was serving at the time. No one in the wider school community had any idea of what I was attempting. It worked! So I told the administration what I had done and asked permission to expand to a pilot in ten schools. The school administrators did not think, at first, that ten schools would be interested; however, I already had ten schools *asking* to be in the pilot. The rest, as the expression goes, is history. Having achieved enormous successes for children and their families, we march on.

I am truly hoping that after "getting your marching orders" from reading this book, you too will be ready to march on—for the kids. I will assist you in any way possible. Together, let's begin!

If you have been taking the Forward Actions suggested at the end of each chapter, you already have part of the work done.

Take these 11 important steps now!

1. Make a list of supportive personal and professional relationships (Forward Actions, Chapter 2).

2. Decide how this process can best be flexed to fit the needs of children in your jurisdiction.

3. Review the material presented in Chapter 7, and then choose the individual school or school division staff member to whom you'll first present your plans.

4. Identify your stakeholders and get commitments from them for a simple pilot program (three elementary schools worked well for our school division).

    NOTE: *How you present the knowledge you've gathered that is relevant to your particular locale makes all the difference!*

5. Always have appropriate documentation when you present—and always document what is transpiring.

6. Do your homework! Prior to meeting as a small group, put into writing what you believe the shared goal(s) must be; use materials provided in this book to familiarize yourself with building collaborative skills.

7. Set up an initial meeting of basic stakeholders. Be sure to set the tone for the future at the very beginning of the meeting by focusing on what *can* be accomplished through the CFK process. Encourage only positive interactions.

8. Have an agenda and visual aids.

9. Share the undeniable research; clearly delineate the benefits of this early-intervention program.

10. Obtain commitments to implement the pilot program.

11. Set another meeting date and time.

You are now off and running! You're ready to discuss establishing a common language, training, Teams, collaboration concepts, open communication, productive listening, confidentiality, referral process, Team meeting protocol, and more. All of the things you've read about in this book will help you help children and families move toward real success.

Use the model on the following pages to assist in the start-up process.

Collaboration For Kids
Advocating for Children Through Multi-Agency Collaboration: an Early-Intervention Model

TO BEGIN

- Start small: agencies and 1–3 schools.

- The "lead" person needs to be one who has a true passion for the well-being of children—who shines with dedication and energy.

- The lead person will make all initial contacts and disperse all initial information to participating agencies and schools.

- Initial agencies will include Social Services, Mental Health, Court Services, and Cooperative Extension.

- Connect first with schools (school division supervisor, principal, school social worker, guidance counselor = key players). Promote enthusiasm for early-intervention principles.

CONTACT INDIVIDUALS DIRECTLY

Individual contacts prior to any group meeting work best. Be prepared with something in print and a PowerPoint or other *simple* presentation. Share with each the following:

- Research

- Theory and benefits of early intervention

- Importance of collaborative training

- No Child Left Behind data

- National and local indicators

- Benefits of such collaboration

- Proven results of such a program

Reach agreement on *local need, collaborative process,* and *participation in a pilot.* Use local and national statistics to demonstrate the rises in homelessness, poverty, domestic violence, child abuse and neglect, parental mental health issues, substance abuse, and limited English proficiency.

OBSTACLES TO SUCCESS

The primary obstacle to success is closed-mindedness, a "disease" that is prevalent and at times even contagious. It sounds like this:

- "We don't have the funding to support this kind of thing."

- "Our people are already overloaded and don't have time for this."

- "We take care of our own; we don't need any other programs" (isolation in work practices and territorial beliefs).

- "We already collaborate" (lack of understanding of the concepts of collaboration).

- "Sorry, too busy to let you know" (need for better communication, communication, communication ...).

PROGRAM BENEFITS FOR ALL

- Stabilized families with follow-through support and monitoring

- Reduced family violence

- Reduced truancy and tardiness

- Increased academic success

- Improved home and school behaviors for children and parents

- More appropriate use of community resources and services

- Reduced school and community violence

- Healthier family systems

- Likely reduced court-case intake for older children

TRAINING THE INITIAL PARTICIPANTS*

By reading this book, you have shown an interest in making a difference in the lives of children and families, as well as in the safety and security of your community. Now it is time to take the forward actions we have discussed here. This proven CFK process is not complex, expensive, or scary. It is simply what is needed.

I frequently find myself repeating my belief that children have a right to be safe, a right to be nurtured and loved, and a right to be educated. I feel this strongly enough to offer you my assistance in beginning your CFK pilot program. Here is my e-mail address for this purpose: collaborationforkids@gmail.com.

In closing, allow me to remind you of how we began.

FACT: Research and statistics demonstrate that the number of children "unavailable to learn" due to issues outside of school continues to increase daily.

FORWARD ACTIONS

- Believe that change is possible!

- Care passionately!

- Communicate positively!

- Listen productively!

- Move forward with action, now!

* Subjects to cover are listed in Chapter 6.

EPILOGUE

It isn't news to anyone that we're living in a fast-paced world. People working in our various human service systems often feel under funded and over-scheduled. Frequently, only brief snapshots of children's very real, complex, long-standing problems can be obtained. Unfortunately, this approach doesn't always serve well, as children can be quite easily misrepresented and misunderstood. To be sure, one cannot adequately assign appropriate protective measures following one 15-minute interview with an abused child and one 30-minute interview with the suspected parent. What you observe in one home visit cannot adequately illustrate a dysfunctional or dangerous home situation that has existed for months—or even generations. You cannot represent a child's best interest in court after examining the case for the first time for ten minutes in the halls of the courthouse. You cannot teach a child who is chronically hungry and tired. You cannot educate a child who has missed 35 days of school for reasons that aren't clear to anyone on the staff.

A snapshot of circumstances will never be adequate when it comes to a child's education, safety, or well-being. We must have the whole panoramic picture in order to determine what is needed. This is not happening in most areas of the United States, but it is what CFK provides, over time, for every child involved. Everyone works together through an early-intervention process, in *true* collaboration for the best interest of the whole child.

I wish you the greatest success!

Heatherly Woods Conway, Ed.D.

USING THE CD

The CD that comes with this book is provided to make Collaboration For Kids information and forms more easily available to the reader. These materials can be copied and used to present the idea of the program, and its successful record, to your potential collaborators.

On the disk you'll find the Introduction Packet, containing the two-page handout, the year-to-year report, the judge's letter documenting his belief that the number of court cases has been reduced as a result of the Prince William County program, letters from principals stating why they support the program's continuation, the Memorandum of Understanding establishing CFK (CCS) as a formal entity in Prince William County, and two sample newsletters from the existing program. Also included are the sample Glossary of Terms, a list of resources to explore, the entire CFK Referral Packet, the Team Action Plan form, the survey forms (parent and stakeholder), and the sample statistics form.

Finally, you'll find a list that tells you how to begin, things to include when making contacts, some of the obstacles you might encounter, and the benefits that result from the CFK program.

Appendix

If your actions inspire others to dream more,
learn more, do more and become more, you are a leader.

–John Quincy Adams
Sixth president of the United States

WILLIAM ALAN BECKER

JANICE JUSTINA BRICE

PAUL F. GLUCHOWSKI

JAMES B. ROBESON

MARY GRACE O'BRIEN

Raymond O. Kellam
1922-1990

Patrick D. Molinari
1937-1998

JUDGES

COMMONWEALTH of VIRGINIA

Thirty-first District
Juvenile and Domestic Relations District Court
9311 LEE AVENUE
MANASSAS, VIRGINIA 20110
TELEPHONE: (703) 792-6160
FAX NO. (703) 792-7863

November 30, 2004

FRANCES H. HEDRICK
CLERK OF COURT

SERVING:
PRINCE WILLIAM COUNTY
CITIES OF MANASSAS &
MANASSAS PARK

Thomas Carter
Director of Special Education
Prince William County Public Schools
P.O. Box 389
Manassas, Virginia 20108

Re: Comprehensive Child Study Program

Dear Mr. Carter:

On behalf of the judges of this court, I want to express our appreciation to you and your staff for giving us a brief update on the Comprehensive Child Study Program. Many of us remember the initial briefing when the program was just beginning. We are delighted to hear of its continued success and of the expansion to so many additional schools.

As was mentioned at our meeting, our only reservation was the conservative estimates regarding the positive impact on the other children who share a classroom with a child referred to your program. My colleagues and I are convinced that your program has resulted in widespread improvement in classroom environments since at-risk-children and their families have early access to appropriate family services. Although we are not able to provide any empirical data, we believe your program has also resulted in fewer children and families appearing in our court.

Best wishes for continued success with this most significant early intervention opportunity for the children of our community.

Sincerely,

William Alan Becker

Antietam Elementary School
12000 Antietam Road • Lake Ridge, Virginia 22192
(703) 497-7619 • Fax: (703) 491-7603

Angela Atwater
Principal
atwateag@pwcs.edu

Virginia Ripperger
Assistant Principal
rippervl@pwcs.edu

December 9, 2003

Dear Mrs. Gauch,

I write this letter in support of the Comprehensive Child Study Program. Antietam Elementary has participated in CCS for 3 years. During this time, Pam Trapp and her members have consistently been available to meet with families in need. Their expertise has helped families in crisis in ways that we are not equipped to. For example, when a young family was devastated by the untimely death of the father, Pam and her committee stepped in and helped the mother regain control. This year, a new student registered at Antietam. This is a child with extreme anxiety that was preventing him from attending school on a consistent basis. With the help of CCS, we have been able to help this student attend school regularly as well as help the family enroll in some much needed family counseling.

Last week we experienced an unforunate incident involving a man who entered our school under the influence. Luckily, no one was hurt. However, upon speaking with the mother the next day, I was informed that the couple is planning to stay together, but the mother is awaiting test results because the boyfriend has been in the company of an HIV positive drug dealer. This mother came to me begging for help. She recognized that she needed to get tested immediately, but had no idea how to go about seeking aid for medical assistance, information concerning the judicial system and help for her two young daughters. Immediately I thought of the Comprehensive Child Study Program. When I called Pam, she was prepared to coordinate her team and rally around this family ASAP! These are just 3 examples of the many times CCS has responded to our call.

In closing, I cannot say how much I appreciate and support this program. I have found the members to be professional, caring and responsive. I hope the county will consider making CCS a line item on the school board budget. As a public school with a diverse and ever-changing student population, we recognize that in order to educate the child, there are times that it is necessary to "wrap around" a family in need to achieve that goal. Comprehensive Child Study does just that, allowing the child to receive the education and security that every child deserves.

With much thanks,

Angela Atwater

Angela Atwater,
Principal

cc: Jenny Bovard
    Pam Trapp

From: Pam Gauch
To: Wayne Ralston
Date: 12/3/03 12:54PM
Subject: Re: Comprehensive Child Study

Wayne,

  Thank you for your email about Comprehensive Child Study. I share your views and have included it in my budget recommendations for next year! I appreciate your interest in this program. It's good to hear from someone who is implementing the program firsthand and who can realize the benefits it brings to children. I will use some of your feedback as I discuss this with the superintendent's staff and the school board. Thanks! Pam

Pamela K. Gauch
Associate Superintendent for Instruction
Prince William County Public Schools
P.O. Box 389
Manassas, VA 20108
703-791-8710
gauchpk@pwcs.edu

>>> Wayne Ralston 12/02/03 04:32PM >>>
Dear Mrs. Gauch,

  This letter is to encourage you to make every effort to include the Comprehensive Child Study (CCS) program in the coming year's budget. I have had the opportunity to watch this important program grow from a tiny beginning with three schools in the 1998-1999 school year to thirty-nine schools this school year.

  This is a program that is meeting a critical need in the community. In the many schools I have served in during my years in Prince William County, I have seen real needs brought to the table in meetings, but then attempts to connect children with critical services have failed. There has been a disconnect, or more accurately a non-connect, as well-intentioned people tried to make the right contacts.

  CCS is an inspired, but logically simple solution. The CCS people bring the children (actually, their parents) and key agencies from Prince William
County (Social Services, Community Services Board, Court Services, Health Department, Pediatric Primary Care, Cooperative Extension, Turning Points, and/or Volunteer Emergency Families for Children) together - at the same table. Instead of saying, "Prince William County Mental Health Services can help you", and leaving the success of the solution pending successful connection of the parties, the CCS meeting can say to the families, "Okay. Here are the people from Prince William County Mental Health Services. How can you work together and when will you do it?"

  This is a program that is making a positive difference for our students day in and day out. Thirty-nine schools have seen the importance of this program for their students. It is time that every child in the school system has access to the program.

  The experimental program has succeeded beyond expectations. Like the "mobile health vans" in the eastern end of the county, this program is making life better(and education more successful) for children and their families. We need to make it a permanent part of our educational program.
                                      Respectfully,
                                      Wayne Ralston

Comprehensive Child Study Program

Memorandum of Understanding

Among

**Prince William County Schools (Comprehensive Child Study Program),
Prince William County Department of Social Services,
Prince William County Community Services Board,
31st Judicial District Court Services Unit, and
Virginia Cooperative Extension.**

In order to facilitate cooperation among the Prince William County School Division's Comprehensive Child Study Program, Prince William County Department of Social Services, Prince William County Community Services Board, 31st Judicial District Court Services Unit, and Virginia Cooperative Extension, this Memorandum of Understanding was developed. This document will be in effect from January 15, 2005 to January 15, 2010. It can be reviewed upon request of any of the participants or as a part of the Comprehensive Child Study Five Year Plan.

The purpose of this Memorandum of Understanding is to provide maximum communication, coordination, collaboration, and utilization in addressing the needs of Prince William County's high risk children (preschool through grade 5) and their families. In addition, this Memorandum of Understanding recognizes the multi-disciplinary multi-agency Comprehensive Child Study Program (hereafter referred to as the CCS Program), and the *Comprehensive Child Study Action Plan* as viable working professional entities in Prince William County.

The Prince William County School Division and the Comprehensive Child Study Staff shall administer the CCS Program and will:

1. Provide professional staff, offices, and the primary funding for the purpose of coordinating the CCS Program;
2. Utilize the CCS Program to serve children preschool through grade 5 in any elementary school electing to participate;
3. Provide adequate space in participating schools for CCS Team meetings;
4. Provide all CCS program training, forms, and procedures;
5. Maintain statistical tracking and reporting through the Prince William County Schools Office of Planning and Assessment; and
6. Schedule and facilitate team meetings in the schools.

As collaborating agencies, Prince William County Schools (Comprehensive Child Study Program), Prince William County Department of Social Services, Prince William County Community Services Board, 31st Judicial District Court Service Unit, and Virginia Cooperative Extension shall participate actively in maintaining Comprehensive Child Study Program viability and will:

1. Provide staff to participate on CCS Teams;
2. Participate in ongoing training, as needed;
3. Facilitate open and regular communication and collaboration;
4. Utilize and honor the "universal" Release of Information form previously approved by all agencies in Prince William County;
5. Recognize the *Comprehensive Child Study Action Plan* as a viable and valid working document created through the collaboration of a multi agency multidisciplinary team of professionals;
6. Facilitate referrals from CCS to their respective Intake systems;
7. Maintain and share an ongoing awareness of possible funding sources as well as provide referral information and resource data;
8. Facilitate and accept reasonable and appropriate case management, co-management, and referral responsibilities of CCS involved cases;
9. Utilize collaborative communication within organizations to keep all professionals informed of the CCS program and process; and
10. Maintain communication with collaborators involved in a case prior to closing the case.

Edward Kelly, Superintendent
P.W. County Schools   Date_____

Thomas Geib, Director
P.W. County Community Services Board   Date_____

James D. Rankin Jr., Director
31st District Court Services Unit   Date_____

Deborah Carter, Director
Virginia Cooperative Extension   Date_____

Keith Sykes, Director
P.W. County Dept. of Social Services   Date_____

Volume 1, Issue 1

January 2005

THE CONNECTION

The Twice Yearly Newsletter of Comprehensive Child Study

"THE CARNEGIE TASK FORCE ON EDUCATION CONCLUDED: "WHEN THE NEEDS OF THE CHILD DIRECTLY AFFECT LEARNING, THE SCHOOLS MUST MEET THE CHALLENGE."

"IF WE ARE TO REACH REAL PEACE IN THE WORLD, WE SHALL HAVE TO BEGIN WITH THE CHILDREN."

GANDHI

Special points of interest:

- The Comprehensive Child Study Program received the Superintendent's Staff Recognition Team Performance Award in May 2004. Supporting this recognition were letters of praise from parents and human service agencies.

- During the 04-05 school year, training and update presentations have been made to Child Study Teams in the participating schools as well as to Court Service Intake, the Juvenile Court Judges, and the Prince William County Board of Social Services. Included in the audience were representatives from SERVE, Independence Empowerment Center, VA Cooperative Extensions, Brain Injury Services, Butler Community Resource Center, Good Shepherd Housing, Foundation, ACTS, Interfaith Caregivers, Northern VA Family Services, Resource Mothers. Presentations were also made to many Prince William County School Departments as well as all Agency Directors.

- CCS applied for and received confirmation of a Title IV-E grant for the purpose of purchasing office equipment and obtaining consultative services for the development of an Memorandum Of Understanding among agencies as well as the development of a five-year-plan for CCS. As fate would have it, these funds were not forthcoming due to a freeze on Title IV-E funds.

- CCS and DSS continue to closely collaborate on a Title IV-E project that may result in reimbursement for situation specific case management services.

Do You Recall?

As we begin our first newsletter, we would like to remind you of the purpose of the Comprehensive Child Study (CCS) Program. As an early intervention initiative of Prince William County Schools, CCS serves children preschool through grade five, addressing those issues that prevent learning and destabilize families. Currently, in 44 elementary schools, CCS is now in its seventh successful year as a proactive collaboration of the school division and all Prince William County human service agencies. Working in trained Teams within the schools, CCS offers support, positive assistance, and services to children and families. The number of children who are "unavailable to learn" due to issues outside of school continues to be on the rise across the nation and in Prince William County. CCS acts to lower these numbers and create successful learners and citizens.

CCS Action Plan

People actively working with children, will be hearing the term *CCS Action Plan*. This Plan is one that is formed in the CCS Team meeting with the parent(s) participating. It is an individualized monitored plan that identifies and develops resources and services needed to move the child and family toward specific needed goals that will insure learning and stabilization. This plan is recognized as a viable working document by the School Division, Department of Social Services, Community Services Board, Court Services Unit, and the Juvenile Court Judges.

Recent correspondence received by the Director of Special Education from the Judges of the Juvenile Courts stated, "My colleagues and I are convinced that your program (CCS) has resulted in widespread improvement in classroom environments since at-risk children and their families have early access to appropriate family services. **Although we are not able to provide any empirical data, we believe your program has also resulted in fewer children and families appearing in our court.**"

Positive Progress For Many

During the 2003-04 school year, positive progress was made for many children and their families. Statistics computed by the Prince William County Schools Office of Planning and Assessment yielded the following:

***Children's issues** at intake included truancy, tardiness, academic and IEP, behavioral, and medical. **Family issues** included child protection, domestic violence, mental health, basic needs, parent compliance and participation, and sudden family emergencies such as house fires or sudden onset of illness.*
    271 cases came to CCS during the '03-'04 school year from 38 schools
    1,533 children were positively impacted by CCS action
    89.1% improvement was documented in at least one area of concern for each child/family

Participating Children:
Regular Education	54%
Special Education	46%
Minority	45.5%
Limited English	5.4%
Free/Reduced Lunch	58.4%

Trends Clearly Noted:
Rise in the number of homeless
Rise in the number of working poor
Rise in child protection and domestic violence issues
Rise in adult substance abuse and alcoholism
Rise in child and parent mental health issues
Rise in unusual childhood syndromes

Referrals for 5th Graders

Referrals to CCS for fifth graders will not be accepted after March 1 of this school year. CCS is an early intervention K-5 program, and we do not have the staff to follow fifth graders into middle school. If a fifth grade student is referred to us by March 1, we have several months to coordinate the needed services, which can then be monitored by the middle school. We will still be available for consultations regarding fifth graders through the end of the school year.

Collaboration

The passion and hard work demonstrated by all individuals who make up our CCS Team is quite an amazing thing to behold. Their collaborative effort toward improving the lives and learning of Prince William's children is exemplary, and the CCS staff offers their gratitude for such dedication.

Collaboration Grows Stronger

A primary goal of CCS for the 04-05 school year has been to create a Memorandum of Understanding among the participating CCS stake holders. This Memorandum has now been completed and is in the process of being signed by all. Signatories include the Superintendent of Schools and the Directors of the Department of Social Services, Community Services Board, Court Service Unit, and VA Cooperative Extension. We thank the participants who worked on the Memorandum of Understanding for their guidance and input.

Upcoming, will be the construction of a working Five Year Plan for the CCS Program.

pwcs.edu

THE CONNECTION

The Twice Yearly Newsletter of Comprehensive Child Study

Volume 1, Issue 2

June 2005

"OURS IS NOT THE TASK OF FIXING THE ENTIRE WORLD ALL AT ONCE, BUT OF STRETCHING OUT TO MEND THE PART OF THE WORLD THAT IS WITHIN OUR REACH." ESTES

Community Partners

CCS would like to thank all of our community partners for their continued dedication and hard work. During the 2004-2005 school year we have seen an increase in the complexity of the cases that were brought to CCS. This has required more collaboration and creative approaches to address the needs of children and families. Although all of us have experienced personal and professional demands that at times have stretched us thin, we continue to work together as a Team.

"Your words and thoughts have the power to create change so pay attention."
Author Unknown

CCS and Head Start Build a Bridge

As we all know, the Head Start preschool program provides a wonderful opportunity for children and families to establish a positive early learning foundation and encourages family participation. Family service workers assist each family in accessing services that the child might need.

Comprehensive Child Study (CCS), working with children kindergarten through grade five, also works to connect families with resources so these children may be fully available to learn and grow.

Until recently there has been no bridge between these two programs. In many cases the supports that were provided in the Head Start program help the child to transition into kindergarten. In other cases, the children and their families are unable to sustain the momentum established. Over the years we have seen these same children resurface due to behavior problems, ongoing mental health issues, difficult family dynamics, and academic concerns.

CCS and Head Start Family Support Workers are now joining together to create the needed bridge for those children and families about to enter kindergarten who need ongoing support. CCS through resources, support services, and coordination with the schools will work with the identified students and families toward ensuring that no child is left behind.

CCS Welcomes New Specialist

As we publish our last newsletter for this school year, we are proud to welcome Colleen "Kai" Munster aboard as a new part-time Comprehensive Child Study Specialist. Kai joined us in February as we grew from 37 to 44 participating schools. In the few months that she has been a part of the CCS program she has more than demonstrated her dedication and passion for helping children and families. Her knowledge and professionalism is deeply appreciated by all who have worked with her. Previously, Kai worked for Prince William County Schools as a Visiting Teacher.

"Begin with the end in mind." Covey

Time is of the Essence When it Comes to Referrals

CCS has always been the next step, when Child Study intervention and school resources have been tried. CCS is a process and we encourage schools to discuss cases with us. Together we can identify possible school based options or develop a plan to move forward to CCS. Although CCS is not an emergency intervention, the earlier CCS becomes involved, the more opportunity there is to provide assistance and prevent further escalation of the identified concerns. Please know that CCS, as a multi-disciplinary team, appreciates how very much you do for children in the schools. Our community partners in CCS have repeatedly expressed their appreciation and respect for school employees and all that is done to enhance the learning environment and process for the benefit of the children.

CCS to Present at Governor's Conference

It is with great pride that CCS has accepted an invitation to present at the 2005 Governor's Conference on Education. The conference will he held on July 19 in the grand Ballroom of the Richmond Marriott. Pam Trapp and Heather Conway will give four presentations during the conference describing, the history, purpose and goals of CCS, how community collaboration evolves, what training is involved in starting such a program, the obvious need for the program and the success created for children and families through early intervention. Also emphasized will be what happens if appropriate early intervention is not available.

2004-2005 Participating Schools

Ann Ludwig	Montclair
Antietam	Mullen
Bel-Air	Neabsco
Belmont	Nokesville
Bennett	Occoquan
Child Find	Old Bridge
Coles	Pattie
Dale City	Penn
Dumfries	Potomac View
Ellis	River Oaks
Enterprise	Signal Hill
Featherstone	Sinclair
Kerrydale	Springwoods
Kilby	Sudley
King	Swans Creek
Lake Ridge	Triangle
Leesylvania	Tyler
Loch Lomond	Vaughan
Marshall	West Gate
Mary Williams	Westridge
Marumsco Hills	Yorkshire
McAuliffe	
Minnieville	

Busy Year!

It has been a busy year for CCS. CCS Specialists have been involved in a variety of endeavors: Harmony, Kindergarten Behavior Task Force, Neurofeedback Training, Family Group Decision Making as well as the development of a Memorandum of Understanding among CCS participating agencies.

This year, the intensity and complexity of the cases referred presented challenges and pushed the collaboration process to new levels. Cases involving multiple medical issues, CPS concerns, mental health, family violence and behavioral issues all impacted the educational progress. Coordination and resource develop to address these needs required extensive work and collaboration.

Contacts

The effective use of the CCS process has been beneficial to many students and families as well as school personnel. We appreciate the following administrators who have agreed to be contacts for their peers to discuss CCS and how it has worked for them. Angie Atwater, Linda Dockery, Jarcelynn Hart, Michele Salzano, Joyce Sigmundsson, Linda Trexler and Jane Wheeless, and Damon Cerrone.

Planning is the key to tasks that get finished." Payne

BIBLIOGRAPHY

When you know that your thoughts expand into action,
you become very careful about what you think ...

–Wayne W. Dyer
Author and psychotherapist

BY AGENCY

Family Connection Partnership. (2002). *Navigating the Collaborative Process: An Introduction to Collaboration.* Atlanta, GA: 2V-Navigation, the Collaborative Process.

BY AUTHOR

Arnow, J. (1995). *Teaching Peace.* Berkeley, CA: Perigree Books.

Aquirre, L.M. (1995). California's efforts toward school-linked, integrated, comprehensive services. *Social Work in Education,* 17 (4), 217–225.

Barth, R.P. (1985). Collaboration between child welfare and school social work services. *Social Work in Education,* 8 (1), 32–47.

Berrick, J.D., & Barth, R.P. (1991). The role of the school social worker in child abuse prevention. *Social Work in Education,* 13 (3), 195–202.

Bridgeland, W.M., & Duane, E.A. (1993). Child abuse intervention: the accused, the schools and protective services. *Education,* 114 (1), 113–120.

Carnegie Task Force on Education in the Primary Grades. (1994). *Years of Promise: A Comprehensive Learning Strategy for America's Children.* New York, NY: Carnegie Corporation.

Cheney & Company of New Haven, CT (Eds.). (1992). *The essential components of a successful education: putting policy into practice.* Washington, DC: Business Roundtable.

Children's Defense Fund. (2003). *National Kids Count: A Data Book.* Washington, DC: Children's Defense Fund.

Conway, H.W. (1998). Children unavailable: a critical analysis of collaboration between school professionals and child protective services in issues of child abuse and neglect. Ed.D. dissertation. California Coast University.

Costen, L.B., Karger, H., & Stoesz, D. (1996). *The Politics of Child Abuse in America*. New York, NY: Oxford University Press.

Cryan, J.R. (1985). Intellectual, emotional, and social deficits of abused children: A review. *Childhood Education, 61*, 388–392.

DeVol, P.E. (2004). *Getting Ahead in a Just-Gettin'-By World: Building Your Resources for a Better Life*. Highlands, TX: aha! Process.

Dryfoos, J.G. (1998). *Full-Service Schools*. San Francisco, CA: Jossey-Bass Publishers.

Dryfoos, J.G., & Maguire, S. (2002). *Inside Full-Service Community Schools*. San Francisco, CA: Jossey-Bass Publishers.

Dyer, W.W. (1995). *Your Sacred Self*. New York, NY: HarperCollins.

Fead, A.K. (1985). *The Child Abuse Crisis: Impact on the Schools*. Arlington, VA: Capitol Publications.

Finkelhor, D., Hotaling, G., & Yllo, K. (1988). *Stopping Family Violence: Research Priorities for the Coming Decade*. Newbury Park, CA: Sage Publications.

Fogg, D.C. (1994). *Team-Based Strategic Planning: A Complete Guide to Structuring, Facilitating, and Implementing the Process*. Washington, DC: Amacom.

Garbarino, J., Dubrow, N., Kostelny, K., & Pardo, C. (1992). *Children in Danger*. San Francisco, CA: Jossey-Bass Publishers.

Garner, H.G. (1995). *Teamwork Models and Experience in Education*. Boston, MA: Allyn & Bacon.

Garner, H.G. (2000). *Helping Others Through Teamwork* (Second Edition). Atlanta, GA: CWLA Press.

Gaudin, J.M. (1993). *Child Neglect: A Guide for Intervention*. Washington, DC: Department of Health & Human Services.

Goleman, D. (1995). *Emotional Intelligence*. New York, NY: Bantam Books.

Goodlad, J. (1994). *What Schools Are For* (Second Edition). Bloomington, IN: Phi Delta Kappa Educational Foundation.

Haase, C.C., & Kempe, R.S. (1990). The school and protective services. *Education and Urban Society*, 22, 258–269.

Hjorth, C.W., & Ostrov, E. (1982). The self-image of physically abused adolescents.

Jehl, J., & Krist, M. (1992). Getting ready to provide school-linked services: What schools must do. Behrman, R.E. (Ed.), *The Future of Children: School-linked Services*, 2 (1), 95–106.

Kretzman, J.P., & McKnight, J.L. (1993). *Building Communities from the Inside Out*. Chicago, IL: ACTA Publications.

Kurtz, P.D., Gaudin, J.M. Jr., Wodarski J.S., & Howing, P.T. (1993). Maltreatment and the school-aged child: School performance consequences. *Child Abuse and Neglect*, 17, 581–589.

Maeroff, G.I. (1993). *Team Building for School Change: Equipping Teachers for New Roles*. New York, NY: Teachers College Press.

Martinez, R.J. (1992). Matching services with needs. *Thrust for Educational Leadership*, 32–35. January.

Mattessich, P.W., & Monsey, B.R. (1992). *Collaboration: What Makes It Work*. St. Paul, MN: Amherst H. Wilder Foundation.

Melaville, A.I., & Blank, M.J. (1991). *What it takes: structuring interagency partnerships to connect children and families with comprehensive services*. Washington, DC: Education and Human Services Consortium. August.

Miranda, L.C. (1991). *Latino Child Poverty in the United States*. Washington, DC: Children's Defense Fund.

Mulroy, E.A. (1997). Building a neighborhood network: interorganizational collaboration to prevent child abuse and neglect. *Social Work*, 42, 225–264.

O'Callaghan, J.B. (1993). *School-Based Collaboration with Families: Constructing Family-School-Agency Partnerships That Work*. San Francisco, CA: Jossey-Bass Publishers.

Olsen, W.R., & Sommers, W.A. (2004). *A Trainer's Companion: Stories to Stimulate Reflection, Conversation, Action*. Highlands, TX: aha! Process.

Palmer, P. (1998). *The Courage to Teach*. San Francisco, CA: Jossey-Bass Publishers.

Payne, R.K. (2005). *A Framework for Understanding Poverty* (Fifth Edition). Highlands, TX: aha! Process.

Payne, R.K., DeVol, P.E., & Dreussi Smith, T. (2006). *Bridges Out of Poverty: Strategies for Professionals and Communities* (Third Edition). Highlands, TX: aha! Process.

Pirez, S. (2002). *Building Systems of Care: A Primer.* National Technical Assistance Center for Children's Mental Health. Washington, DC: Georgetown University.

Plotkin, D., & Twentyman, C.T. (1992). A multimodel assessment of behavioral and cognitive deficits in abused and neglected preschoolers. *Child Development,* 55, 794–802.

Quint, S. (1994). *Schooling Homeless Children.* New York, NY: Teachers College Press.

Raley, G.A. (1997). *The New Community Collaboration Manual.* Washington, DC: National Assembly.

Schaps, E., & Watson, M., (1996). Schools as caring communities. *Virginia Journal of Education,* 89 (4), 7–11. January.

Sedlak, A.J., & Broadhurst, D.D. (1996). *The Third National Incidence Study of Child Abuse and Neglect.* Washington, DC: Department of Health & Human Services.

Topchik, G. (2004). *The Accidental Manager.* New York, NY: Silver Star Enterprises.

Wentworth, E. (1992). *Agents of change.* Washington, DC: Business Roundtable.

BY PUBLICATION

Journal of Youth and Adolescence, 11 (2), 71–76.

BY WEBSITE

www.d.umn.edu: Student Handbook: "Listening Skills."

www.infoplease.com: "Listening Skills."

www.kidsource.com: "How Can Parents Model Good Listening Skills." Carl Smith.

WE'D LIKE TO HEAR FROM YOU!

 **Join us on Facebook**
www.facebook.com/rubypayne

 **Respond to our blog**
www.ahaprocess.com/blog

 **Subscribe to our YouTube channel**
www.youtube.com/ahaprocess

 **Download Free Resources**
www.ahaprocess.com

- **Visit our online store for related titles at www.ahaprocess.com/store**
- **Download an eBook**
- **Sign up for a one-hour SHORT COURSE online**

aha! Process, Inc.

Interventions

Engage and Graduate Your Secondary Students: Preventing Dropouts

Audience: Recommended for teachers and administrators grades 7–12.

Needs/issues/problems addressed:
- Poverty
- Achievement gap
- Attendance/truancy
- Dropouts

Workshop Description:
This workshop is for educators in grades 7–12 who want to design programs for student success with special emphasis on under-resourced learners.

Research-Based Strategies

Audience: Recommended for instructional staff (teachers, classroom paraprofessionals).

Needs/issues/problems addressed:
- Poverty
- Achievement gap
- Response to Intervention (RTI)

Workshop Description:
A teacher-friendly workshop focused on serving under-resourced students, Research-Based Strategies provides educators with hands-on techniques that help them narrow and then eliminate the achievement gap for all students, but especially under-resourced students.

Response to Intervention (RTI)

Audience: Recommended for K–12 teachers and administrators.

Needs/issues/problems addressed:
- Achievement gap
- Special education

Workshop Description:
Learn about the "what," the "why," and the "how" of Response to Intervention (RTI) and the under-resourced learner.

Consulting/Academic Coaching

Audience: Recommended for K–12 educators.

Needs/issues/problems addressed:
- Achievement gap and accountability requirements
- Alternative school students
- Poverty/Title I

Description:
Academic coaching is the follow-up and support provided to teachers through small group meetings. The small groups may include one or several grade levels at the elementary level, or one or several departments, or content areas at the secondary level.

(800) 424-9484 • www.ahaprocess.com/workshops/